KU-140-562

WRITERS AND CRITICS

Chief Editor
A. NORMAN JEFFARES

Advisory Editors
DAVID DAICHES   C. P. SNOW

WHITMAN is a poet whose vision is of "single lives ennobled and satisfied by sharing the general life of the universe". His ideas and his language convey a view of himself as a corporate poetic being seen in terms of human comedy; his weaknesses and his ability to affirm seize upon death, but death seen as an extension of his passion for life.

Whitman's reputation is being steadily restored and in this revaluation Geoffrey Dutton, who is himself a poet of distinction, plays a part both trenchant and appreciative with this lively perceptive study. He recognises the sheer weight of Whitman's sincerity and stresses his freshness of language and immense human sympathy.

Geoffrey Dutton, an Oxford graduate now lecturing in Adelaide, is an Australian who has travelled widely and adventurously. His *States of the Union* is one of several travel books which record these experiences; his *Founder of a City* deals with Colonel Light's life and role in the foundation of Adelaide; and he is co-editor of the quarterly *Australian Letters* and general editor of *Australian Writers and their Work*.

He writes of Whitman out of a knowledge of the old world and the new; he understands the creation of a national myth; and as a result his criticism of Whitman's achievement arises from a deep understanding of the role of the poet as interpreter of the human identity which is the basis of democracy.

WALT WHITMAN

GEOFFREY DUTTON

OLIVER AND BOYD
EDINBURGH AND LONDON

OLIVER AND BOYD LTD
Tweeddale Court
Edinburgh 1

39A Welbeck Street
London W. 1

First published 1961
Reprinted 1967

Printed in Great Britain for Oliver and Boyd Ltd
by Robert MacLehose and Co. Ltd, Glasgow

CONTENTS

ACKNOWLEDGMENTS

Acknowledgments are due to the following publishers for permission to quote from the works specified: Faber and Faber Ltd (T. S. Eliot, intro. to *Selected Poems of Ezra Pound*); Oxford University Press Ltd (*Letters of Gerard Manley Hopkins to Robert Bridges*, ed. C. C. Abbott); and Martin Secker and Warburg Ltd (Basil de Selincourt, *Walt Whitman, A Critical Study*).

The photograph on the cover is reproduced by courtesy of the Walt Whitman House, Camden, New Jersey.

ABBREVIATED TITLES USED IN THE TEXT

In references to the *Complete Writings of Walt Whitman*, volumes are numbered continuously I–X. The actual volumes are numbered Verse, I–III and Prose, I–VII. Thus VOL. IV is equivalent to Prose, VOL. I; VOL. VII is equivalent to Prose, VOL. IV, and so on.

C.W.	=	*The Complete Writings of Walt Whitman.*
S.S.	=	Gay Wilson Allen, *The Solitary Singer, a Critical Biography of Walt Whitman.*
U.P.P.	=	*Uncollected Poetry and Prose of Walt Whitman,* ed. Emory Holloway.
W.W.C.	=	Horace L. Traubel, *With Walt Whitman in Camden.*

CHAPTER I

THE MAN AND THE PROSE

Walt Whitman's survival has been doubly precarious in an age when the ordinary reader of poetry is often made to feel that he has blundered into the province of the professional, where all is difficult and oblique. In the first place, Whitman's hoped-for audience, democracy *en masse*, wastes as little time on Whitman as on any other poet; secondly, most of the literary pundits of our age either dismiss Whitman or avoid discussing him, however much in secret they may owe to him. His virtues have been out of fashion. Those trained to hunt for irony and ambiguity dodge away from the full-throated voice and sentiments of affirmation; those accustomed to the tortuous self-consciousness of modern psychology are dismayed by the exultations of a pre-Freudian who would rather sing about his weird sex-life than set about explaining it. Those who cherish footnotes and thrive on explications, who relish an embedded quotation from Dante or a sly reference to Confucius or Kierkegaard, resent a poet who said in his old age: "The trouble is that writers are too literary—too damned literary."[1] Nor do those who would return to authority and established religion care for a man who asks: "Has anyone fancied he could sit at last under some due authority and rest satisfied with explanations and realize, and be content and full?"[2] And those who claim Whitman for the world revolution may, amongst many other hindrances, stumble on: "I am not afraid of conservatism, not afraid of going too slow, of being held back."[3]

On the other side, Whitman's defenders present a

touching spectacle as they snuffle through his works
hunting for proofs that he knew evil, doubt, and the
despair of illusions, that he was morbidly fascinated by
wounds and death, that he could be witty, symbolic, and
ambiguous with the best of them. His passport to contemporary fashion is stamped by Jules Laforgue, who
translated some of his poems, and by Hopkins, who was
terrified of the extent of Whitman's potential influence
on him. But neither Whitman's life nor his work was
minor, and as with any great figure, each age can take
what it wants from him. The marvel is that Whitman has
so much to offer, now; so much to which one can apply
his own words: "How curious! how real!"

At best his language is as fresh as words just spoken by
someone you love and as permanent as only the highest
poetic imagination can make it. No passage of time has
corroded the terminals of his sense-perceptions. His
human sympathies are so basic that they are unshakable,
and the great symbols to which his being vibrated are
unchanged and available: the sea, the grass, the song of
a bird, "night, sleep, death and the stars."[4] Even his
optimism is impressive in our disaster-ridden age; he did
not win it easily, nor did he abandon it after the worst
civil war in history. His absurdities and failures are
obvious enough, especially as they are usually uttered
with a prophetic roar. Particularly relevant to an age
which has explored every aspect of personality is Whitman's ceaseless concern with identity; the "myself" and
"you" of his poems make up a highly complex enquiry
into the relations between man's body and soul and the
universe in which he lives, to use Whitman's old-fashioned
but familiar words. The corporate poetic being that
Whitman evolved is primarily a comic one, not laughable
(intentionally, anyhow), but seeing life in terms of human
comedy to which tragedy is incidental, although real
enough. This is where a study of Whitman's life is important. There was insanity in his family; he was sexually

abnormal; his poems were attacked or ignored by most American readers; his experiences in the war moved him profoundly. Despite all this, bitterness and tragedy seemed to him the easy way out. He did not evade them—

> I am the man, I suffer'd, I was there. . . .
> Agonies are one of my changes of garments[5]

—but, together with his understanding and his imagination, he possessed the dignity and resignation of animals ("They do not sweat and whine about their condition.")[6] No poet has written more passionately about death, but seen in the context of his writing this becomes the inevitable extension of his passion for life, his conviction that "The smallest sprout shows there is really no death."[7]

Whitman seldom talked about death without relating it to birth. He himself was born on 31 May 1819, within sound of the sea, on a small farm at West Hills on Long Island. His father, Walter, worked as a carpenter, as well as farming; he had come down in the world from the solid comfort of his parents and his in-laws. The Whitmans were of English Puritan stock; the Van Velsors (the poet's mother's family) were a mixture of Dutch and Welsh. As a child and youth Walt especially loved the Van Velsor homestead, with "the vast kitchen and ample fireplace and the sitting-room adjoining, the plain furniture, the meals, the house full of merry people, my grandmother Amy's sweet old face in its Quaker cap, my grandfather 'the Major,' jovial, red, stout, with sonorous voice and characteristic physiognomy."[8] A few days before Walt's fourth birthday his father transferred the family to Brooklyn, then a town of about 7,000 people, where he hoped to find more profitable work as a carpenter. From Brooklyn, New York was a ferry-ride away.

The early influences on his life were concentrated and varied, so that he grew up with a sense both of comfort and of unease, of pastoral innocence and the hard simplicities of farming, of the sea, a town and a city. Later in life he estimated that there were

> three leading sources and formative stamps to my own character, now solidified for good or bad, and its subsequent literary and other outgrowth—the maternal nativity-stock brought hither from far-away Netherlands, for one, (doubtless the best)—the subterranean tenacity and central bony structure (obstinacy, wilfulness) which I get from my paternal English elements, for another—and the combination of my Long Island birth-spot, sea-shores, childhood's scenes, absorptions, with teeming Brooklyn and New York— with, I suppose, my experiences afterward in the secession outbreak, for the third.[9]

The mother-image, often merging with that of the sea, is always vital and honoured in his poetry, and the fact that the actual woman, Louisa Whitman, was almost illiterate and certainly never understood her son's poems may help to explain his life-long conviction that literature must never become an end in itself. The father-image, on the other hand, is never satisfactory, and Whitman is forced either to idealise it or to transform and transfer it to himself with a roll of drums, or else throw himself on it in desperation as the land, trailed with drift and *débris*, on which the fierce old sea-mother beats. Nevertheless, he learnt both a trade and many ideas from his father, who had known and venerated Tom Paine, and whose admiration for Elias Hicks, the radical Quaker, added further weight in young Walt's mind to the respect he felt for his maternal Quaker grandmother.

In Whitman's estimate of the sources of his character he does not mention the disruptive elements in his family life. Walter senior's odd practice was to build a house, move in, and then sell it when he had built another. After ten years in Brooklyn he moved the family (but not Walt) back to Long Island, near West Hills. Mrs

Whitman survived ill health to produce nine children. The solidity of their names (Andrew Jackson, George Washington, and Thomas Jefferson were some of them) did not always extend to their lives. The eldest, Jesse, was always unstable, contracted syphilis from an Irish whore, and died in an insane asylum; Walt's favourite sister, Hannah, made a squalid mess of her married life; Andrew became a drunkard, married a slut, and died of tuberculosis of the throat at the age of 36; Eddie, the youngest, was a mentally-defective cripple.

Against all this, Walt was a triumphantly healthy child, with a buoyant nature and a wide world to ramble in, to use one of his favourite words. The landscape of his childhood is like a Brueghel painting, populated with human activity:

As a boy I often went forth with a chum or two, on those frozen fields, with hand-sled, axe and eel-spear, after messes of eels. We would cut holes in the ice, sometimes striking quite an eel-bonanza, and filling our baskets with great, fat, sweet, white-meated fellows.[10]

Forty and more years later the freshness of Long Island had not faded:

the soothing rustle of the waves, and the saline smell— boyhood's times, the clam-digging, bare-foot, and with trowsers roll'd up—hauling down the creek—the perfume of the sedge-meadows—the hay-boat, and the chowder and fishing excursions;—or, of later years, little voyages down and out New York bay, in the pilot boats.[11]

He went for five years, not very systematically, to the public schools, and then at the age of eleven was employed as

a boy in an office, lawyers', father and two sons, Clarke's, Fulton street near Orange. I had a nice desk and window-nook to myself; Edward C. kindly help'd

me at my handwriting and composition, and, (the
signal event of my life up to that time), subscribed for
me to a big circulating library.[12]

Walt read the *Arabian Nights* and the novels and poems
of Walter Scott, and developed a life-long passion for
Scott. In his seventies he said:

> Everything about Scott attracts me: he was one man
> among many men: Scott, Cooper: I go back to them,
> some things in Homer, Aeschylus: then the Bible:
> Byron: Epictetus: they are my daily food: a few others,
> maybe, added.[13]

Shakespeare, for instance, despite his "feudalism";
Shakespeare and Homer in particular Whitman liked
to declaim against the roar of the surf on Long Island's
beaches.

After a short spell working for a doctor, Whitman was
apprenticed to a weekly newspaper and printing office
called the *Long Island Patriot*, and at the age of twelve he
was allowed to contribute "sentimental bits" to the paper.
He continued to learn the trade at other printers',
joined a debating society, went to the New York theatre,
and by the age of 15 or 16 was a healthy fellow as large
and strong as a man. When he was qualified as a journey-
man printer, he went to work for a year or so as a com-
positor in New York; then in 1836 he returned to Long
Island, where, despite his own lack of education, he
became a schoolteacher. He lived under the curious
system as "boarding round," which meant staying for a
day or two in turn at the homes of the parents. This,
however, he considered "one of my best experiences and
deepest lessons in human nature behind the scenes and
in the masses."[14] He continued to teach in what now
seems an extraordinarily desultory fashion for the next
five years, but at the same time he returned to journalism
and founded his own weekly paper, the *Long Islander*.
He wrote, printed, and delivered it himself, and thor-

oughly enjoyed the whole process, but after a year he sold his equipment, and went to work for the editor of the *Long Island Democrat*. Whitman took life easy; the editor's wife did not like him, and thought him lazy. The editor did not mind, even to the extent of having to send the printer's devil to fetch Walt, lying peacefully under an apple tree, to the office; he also printed an essay of Whitman's entitled "How I do love a Loafer." The art of idling was basic to Whitman's character. Although he liked people, he was fundamentally a solitary. Girls did not attract him, nor was he very closely acquainted with any young man of his own age; he dressed conventionally, did not drink or smoke, and the essays and poems he wrote betray no sign of originality or talent beyond the ability of a hack to turn out something in line with contemporary didacticism.

At this period of his life, and indeed at some others later on, it is as if he was existing and waiting, like a great ploughed and sown paddock soaking up the rain and the sun, not to be hurried, needing its due time. Nevertheless, however indolent his mind and body, he did not withdraw from society, and was well embroiled in the 1840 presidential campaign as Democratic electioneer for Queens County; and when he returned to New York in 1841 to work for the *New World*, he made a speech at a Democratic rally. ☺

At the same time, his prestige as a writer increased rapidly by the publication of several stories in the *Democratic Review*; here he was in the company of writers like Poe, Whittier, Bryant, and Hawthorne, although there could be no comparison of quality. "Death in the School-Room (A Fact),"[15] is fairly typical in its melodramatic crudity, the story of a sadistic schoolmaster and a "laughing, good-humor'd" boy, whose countenance is, however, "too unearthly fair for health." The climax comes when the boy goes to sleep in class and Lugare, the master, thrashes the boy's unresponsive shoulders, until in his fury at the child's torpidity he jerks away one of his arms, and the head drops "down on the board with a dull sound." After several well-padded lines about the state of Lugare's countenance the story ends: "Death was in the school-room, and Lugare had been flogging a CORPSE."

Whitman was more at ease when next year he wrote a spirited defence of Dickens called "Boz and Democracy," in which he demolished a critic on the *Globe* who had accused Dickens of immorality in his use of wicked and degrading subject-matter. The critic's opinion was that "To call this the literature of Democracy is to make Democracy as brutal as this gentleman has been pleased to represent it in his native country." Whitman's reply is very relevant to his later views on society and the writer: "A 'democratic writer,' I take it, is one the tendency of whose pages is to destroy those old land-marks which pride and fashion have set up, making impassable distinctions between the brethren of the Great Family. . . . The familiarity with low life wherein Mr Dickens places his readers is a wholesome familiarity."[16] This is an early glimpse of the Whitman, who, thoroughly middle-class though he always remained, would insist on mixing with all types and not being "dainty" about the diseases and horrors of man and society.

Early in 1841 he became editor of the *Aurora*, a small New York daily paper; he lasted less than two months, but such a quick turnover was not unusual for editors at that time. His discharge may have had something to do with habits such as calling in someone else to take over his editorial duties while he took "a stroll on Long Island." However passionately Whitman was embroiled with the life of the city, its crime and comedy—in one of his editorials he attacked the police for "kidnapping" fifty prostitutes in Broadway one evening—he seems always to have needed to take a ferry, real or imaginary, to some place where he could be solitary with nature.

He was soon editing another paper, the *Evening Tattler*, and further stories were appearing in the *Democratic Review*. In 1842 he published an atrocious novel, *Franklin Evans, or the Inebriate,* which ironically enough was his only best-seller. He was later so ashamed of the book that he claimed that he wrote this temperance tract while consuming "a bottle of port or what not," (gin cocktails in another version), a most unlikely proceeding for the abstemious Whitman. He was more honest when he called it "damned rot—rot of the worst sort—not insincere, perhaps, but rot, nevertheless."[17]

Whitman's appearance was always a key to the state of his search for identity; and at this time, as befitting a witty, authoritative and elegant editor, he usually wore "a frock coat and high hat, carried a small cane, and the lapel of his coat was almost invariably ornamented with a boutonniere."[18] In the coarse and brutal New York of the eighteen-forties there is a curious clash between the figure of this dapper editor and the potential democratic poet who is defending Dickens for his honesty in depicting low life. Whitman's editorials got to grips with America as it was, but as yet his imaginative work, in prose or verse, was sentimental and full of bogus morality.

In 1845 Whitman returned to Brooklyn, where his family were also living, having moved back there from the country in 1840; Walt wrote for the Brooklyn *Star* and went for long rambles with his young brother Jeff. In 1846 he took on the most important of his journalistic posts, that of editor of the Brooklyn *Eagle*, a successful and respected Democratic paper in a city that was growing at an enormously quick pace. Whitman remained as editor for nearly two years, and this is the period of his life when he was most clearly the responsible, public-spirited citizen, taking part in politics, concerned about the wages of seamstresses, anxious to see the inhabitants of Oregon, Texas and California enjoying the benefits of American democracy. Close to the wide-open gate of immigration, he was enthusiastically sure that America could offer, not only the possibility of riches, but the certainty of a fuller and happier life than any lived in hidebound Europe. In May 1846 Whitman printed[19] an interview he had had with P. T. Barnum, the great showman, who had recently returned from Europe; Whitman asked him if his trip abroad had made him care less for "Yankeedom." Barnum answered: "My God! no! not a bit of it! Why, sir, you can't imagine the difference.— There everything is frozen—kings and *things*—formal, but absolutely *frozen*: here it is *life*." On a different intellectual level, he had many talks with William Cullen Bryant, who had also recently been in Europe. Together they "took rambles, miles long, till dark, out towards Bedford or Flatbush, in company," and Bryant on these occasions gave Whitman "clear accounts of scenes in Europe—the cities, looks, architecture, art, especially Italy—where he had travel'd a good deal." Whitman's opinions on Europe were clear, even if muffled in journalese: "The old and moth-eaten systems of Europe have had their day, and that evening of their existence which is nigh at hand, will be the token of a glorious dawn for the down-trodden people."[20] A hundred years later, American editors were still writing exactly the same sort of thing; a long evening in Europe seems to be a primary condition of day in America.

Although Whitman was a respectable citizen, conventionally dressed and conscientious in his duties, his habits were as individual as always. In the late afternoon, regularly, one of the apprentices would accompany him to Gray's Swimming Bath; there he swam for twenty minutes, and then took a shower, for which the apprentice worked the pump. Then he would usually head for his favourite relaxations: a ferry-ride to New York, a jaunt down Broadway in an omnibus seated beside the driver, and a visit to the theatre to see a play or opera. He knew all the drivers:

Broadway Jack, Dressmaker, Balky Bill, George Storms, Old Elephant, his brother Young Elephant (who came afterward), Tippy, Pop Rice, Big Frank, Yellow Joe, Pete Callahan, Patsey Dee, and dozens more; for there were hundreds. They had immense qualities, largely animal—eating, drinking; women—great personal pride, in their way—perhaps a few slouches here and there, but I should have trusted the general run of them, in their simple goodwill and honor, under all circumstances. Not only for comradeship, and sometimes affection—great studies I found them also.[21]

In their company he saw "Always something novel or inspiriting; yet mostly to me the hurrying and vast amplitude of those never-ending human currents."

He went to all of Shakespeare's plays that were acted, reading the play carefully the day before, and being swept away by the florid acting of such performers as Mr and Mrs Charles Kean in *King John*. Italian opera was his favourite; in the theatre Whitman's emotions always operated at full steam.

Whitman reviewed many European and American authors in the *Eagle*, reviews that reveal a queer mixture of prissiness when dealing with "coarse" writers and manly disgust with the "sentimental." Queer, that is, only in regard to the developing mind of a great poet; Whitman's attitude is mostly that of an ordinary, conservative, rather puritan American, with a veneration for what nowadays would be called "Mom." He clucked over the novels of Frederika Bremer, which, "depicting in especial the character of *a good, gentle mother*," were "likely to melt and refine the human character."[22]

In 1847 Whitman came more and more into conflict with the political views of the owners of the *Eagle*, and in January 1848 he was once again an unemployed journalist. A few weeks later he was in the lobby of a

New York theatre during an interval and met a man who was about to launch a paper in New Orleans; and according to Whitman, "after fifteen minutes' talk (and a drink)," we made a formal bargain, and he paid me two hundred dollars down to bind the contract and bear my expenses to New Orleans."[23] At last Whitman had his chance to sample some of the vastness of the States. The paper he was to write for was to be called the *Daily Crescent* and the first issue was due early in March, so Whitman had to leave immediately. He took his fourteen-year-old brother Jeff with him, and they made the fortnight's trip by train, stage-coach, Ohio River steamboat, and finally down the Mississippi, Whitman collecting material for a series of sketches which he wrote for the *Crescent*. He stayed in New Orleans for only three months, but various biographers have attempted to make this a crucial episode in Whitman's life, when, liberated by the steamy southern spring and the splendid Creole girls, he is supposed to have had some great sexual experience. There is no evidence at all to support this theory, apart from a fine description of New Orleans octoroons— "women with splendid bodies, no bustles, no corsets, no enormities of any sort; large luminous bright eyes; face a rich olive; habits indolent, yet not lazy as we define laziness North; always more than pretty—'pretty' is too weak a word to apply to them"[24]—and an article defending a performing troupe who made nude tableaux of famous sculptures: "The only objection that we conceive of the undraped figure arises from an assumption of coarseness and grossness intended."[25] What has been used as evidence is the famous letter written to John Addington Symonds in 1890. The English writer had long been wanting some definite statement from the poet he respected so much that the "Calamus" poems were intentionally and unambiguously homosexual in meaning; Symonds himself was entirely sympathetic to such a view. In 1890 Whitman wrote to him:

About the questions on Calamus, etc; they quite daze me. Love is only to be rightly construed by and within its own atmosphere and essential character—all of its pages and pieces so coming strictly under—: that the Calamus part has even allowed the possibility of such construction as mentioned is terrible—I am fain to hope the pp themselves are not to be even mentioned for such gratuitory and quite at the time undreamed and unvouched possibility of morbid inferences which are disavowed by me and seem damnable. . . .

My life, young manhood, mid-age, times South, etc., have been jolly bodily, and doubtless open to criticism. Though unmarried, I have had six children—two are dead—one living Southern grandchild—fine boy writes to me occasionally—circumstances (connected with their benefit and fortune) have separated me from intimate relations.[26]

The first half of this letter and the second have this much in common: they protest too much. For Whitman the idea and the fact were not to be bolted ruthlessly together as they are in our mechanical age. If his obvious homosexuality was sublimated, he wanted it to be left that way; if his approval of parenthood and normal sexuality was questioned, he did not mind inventing a few children of his own as proof. No trace of this casually-scattered brood of six has ever been found. Of course this does not prove their non-existence, but all study of Whitman's life and writings furthers the supposition that he was himself his only subject of sexual experiment. His frankness about masturbation, the most secret of sexual activities, would make it probable that he would be equally frank about any other sexual experiences. Instead, he seems to have shied away from any physical contact more extreme than a kiss.

In his old age he had a most revealing conversation with Traubel about hidden and open sex. After the publication of *Leaves of Grass*, a woman called Susan Garnet Smith, of Hartford, Connecticut, wrote to Whitman offering herself as the mother of his child. Whitman received many odd letters, but this is certainly one of the most extraordinary: ". . . My womb is clean and pure. It is ready for thy child my love. Angels guard the vestibule until thou comest to deposit our and the world's precious treasure. . . ." On the envelope Whitman had written in pencil: "? insane asylum." With justice, Traubel suggested that "You might as well write 'insane' across Children of Adam and the Song of Myself."[27] Susan Smith was doing nothing more than taking Whitman's advice literally. To which Whitman replied: "You are perhaps putting my felt and not said things into words." It was the meaning of the symbol Whitman was concerned with, not its conversion into fact. So did D. H. Lawrence shy back from the women who offered themselves as practice for his theories.

To return to Whitman's New Orleans episode, it is noteworthy that one of his most eloquent short poems, "I saw in Louisana a Live-oak growing," has its origin in that part of the country. The gist of this poem is that Whitman wonders that the tree can "utter joyous leaves, standing alone there without its friend near, for I knew I could not." The twig and the leaves that he breaks off, with a little moss twined around it, "remains to me a curious token, it makes me think of manly love."[28] There is nothing here (or anywhere else) to suggest a welter of paternity in New Orleans.

Whitman's sexuality remains one of his supreme contradictions, and the whole body of his work goes to prove how essential it is for a man to contradict himself. On the one hand, his senses were exquisitely aware; on the other, they were but hints of a further reality:

The real life of my senses and flesh transcending my senses and flesh,

My body done with materials, my sight done with my
material eyes,
Proved to me this day beyond cavil that it is not my
material eyes which finally see,
Nor my material body which finally loves, walks, laughs,
shouts, embraces, procreates.[29]

Here, as in so many instances, Whitman has a great deal
in common with William Blake, the Blake who talked of
the limitations of the Vegetative Eye, and who pro-
claimed that "The man who never changes his opinion
is like standing water, and breeds reptiles of the mind."

After breaking with the management of the *Crescent*,
Whitman went north again, still accompanied by his
brother Jeff. They took various boats up the Mississippi
and the Great Lakes to Chicago, went on to Buffalo and
Niagara Falls, crossed over to Albany and came down the
Hudson to New York.

This round journey was of enormous importance to
Whitman's development, for it was many years before he
made another major excursion into the huge variety of
his country, or sampled its complex development. Time
always meant an extension of space to him, and he now
had from the land a sense of the amplitude he had known
as a child by the sea. He was a big man who needed room,
however much he noticed little things. In fact the oppor-
tunity to sprawl seems to be essential to many major
American writers, just as they need the free movement of
fresh air. Whitman, although fundamentally a dweller
in or near cities, had a mystical faith in the perceptions of
those who live in the open air:

The passionate tenacity of hunters, woodmen, early
risers, cultivators of gardens and orchards and fields,
the love of healthy women for the manly form, sea-
faring persons, drivers of horses, the passion for light
and the open air, all is an old varied sign of the un-
failing perception of beauty, and of a residence of the

poetic in out-door people. They can never be assisted by poets to perceive—some may, but they never can.[30]

In another place he talks of the "roughs and beards and space and ruggedness and nonchalance that the soul loves."[31]

However, in the summer of 1848 Whitman was back again in the atmosphere of journalism and politics. A rival Brooklyn paper, the *Advertizer*, printed a paragraph which said that the true reason for Whitman's rupture with the *Eagle* was that he disagreed with the paper's political principles, and on one occasion kicked a prominent politician down the editorial stairs. The *Eagle's* reply to this makes an amusing comment on Whitman's role as a loafer: "Slow, indolent, heavy, discourteous, and without steady principles. . . . Whoever knows him will laugh at the idea of his *kicking any body*, much less a prominent politician. He is too indolent to kick a musketo."[32]

His spasmodic journalism continued with the editorship of a new paper, the *Weekly Freeman*. This time fate, and not the management, intervened. The day after the first issue a large fire in Brooklyn destroyed his office and equipment; although he did get the paper going again, he resigned from the editorship in September 1849.

At this time he was the owner of a block of land and a house, where he had his family to live with him, as well as using the ground floor as an office. For some time he had been assisting the family with money, and he continued to do so for many years, even when very hard-up himself. For the next few years he seems to have continued in his father's practice of buying and selling houses.

Somehow or another, in the mysterious years between 1849 and 1855 the indolent journalist turned into the astonishing and original poet of *Leaves of Grass*. How it happened remains Whitman's secret; one can imagine him smiling evasively behind one of his many masks and repeating the words of one of his poems:

I will certainly elude you,
Even while you think you had unquestionably caught
me, behold!
Already you see I have escaped from you.[33]

To a certain extent one can chart the influences on his intellect at this time. He was interested in phrenology, had his bumps analysed, and, more important, absorbed some of the jargon of the pseudo-science. He spent a lot of time in the company of artists and sculptors and gave a lecture to the Brooklyn Art Union in which he discussed the relation between beauty and morality. He went frequently to the opera, especially to hear Marietta Alboni; "She used to sweep me away as with whirlwinds." He worked for some time as a carpenter, and abandoned his dandified style of dressing. He visited some of his sick omnibus-driver friends in hospital. One of them, who was "taken sick with the small-pox, had the bad disorder [sc. venereal disease] and was furious with the delirium tremens,"[34] had been his companion in a visit to the World's Fair in the Crystal Palace. At the other extreme of company, he spent a lot of time with Dr Abbott, the proprietor of the Egyptian Museum in Broadway. He also studied books and went to lectures about astronomy. He spent hours in libraries, and filled notebooks with cuttings from books and magazines and his comments on them, the authors ranging from Lucretius to Emerson. The apparent contradictions in his character were being allowed full space to develop; one thing that is certain is that Whitman was not a simple, barbarous, ignorant child of nature, as some of his detractors have tried to paint him. Rather he was in some respects the typical prudent and conscientious nineteenth-century man, believing in self-help, self-education, and self-improvement. Somewhere beneath this humdrum exterior the poetic self was bubbling and about to erupt.

His gradually forming literary theory was deeply influenced by his wide reading of the English literary reviews; Whitman's enthusiasm for America did not blind him to the fact that most of the best products of the English language had come from England. In a review of Monckton Milnes's *Life of Keats*, he marked a quotation from Keats: "A poet is the most unpoetical of anything in existence, because he has no identity; he is continually in for and filling some other body." In the margin Whitman wrote: "The great poet absorbs the identity of others, and the experience of others, and they are definite in him or from him; but he perceives them all through the powerful press of himself."[35] In a way, both Whitman and Keats were saying the same thing.

Meanwhile in his private notebooks he learnt how to let his many selves go, forming some further identity that was not bound by ordinary restraints. "My right hand is time, and my left hand is space. . . . I want the soprano that lithely overleaps the stars, and convulses me like the love-grips of her in whose arms I lay last night . . . dilating me beyond time and air."[36] There is sexual experience of one sort hinted at here; other experiences, more characteristic of Whitman, are elsewhere: "One touch of a tug of me has unhaltered my senses."[37] There is also in these notebook jottings evidence of a liberation of language; this is no mere editorial writer speaking.

In these years he had, in his own words, "to come to himself," and there is no doubt that the greatest literary influence was that of Emerson. "I was simmering, simmering, simmering; Emerson brought me to a boil."[38] The traces of Emerson are often visible in Whitman's work, but more often they are invisible, like the trace elements that make potentially good soil productive. Most important of all, perhaps, is the confidence that Whitman found in Emerson, that a man needs no help of religion, race or caste to discover the extent and power of himself:

Whoso would be a man must be a nonconformist. He

who would gather immortal palms must not be hindered by the name of goodness, but must explore if it be goodness. Nothing is at last sacred but the integrity of your own mind. Absolve you to yourself, and you shall have the suffrage of the world. . . . The other terror that scares us from self-trust is our own consistency. . . . Suppose you contradict yourself; what then? . . . Live ever in a new day. . . . With consistency a great soul has simply nothing to do. . . . To be great is to be misunderstood. . . . Man is timid and apologetic; he is no longer upright; he does not say "I think," "I am," but quotes some saint or sage. He is ashamed before the blade of grass or the blowing rose.[39]

Politically Whitman had always been on the side of the free, democratic individual. In religion he had been influenced by the Quaker belief in the necessity and mystery of the inner self. Having long been concerned with public action, the editorial "we," Whitman was now prepared to go to the source of both action and contemplation, himself. Emerson could also give him a parallel between the infinity of himself and the vastness of nature, in which "Man carries the world in his head, the whole astronomy and chemistry suspended in a thought."[40] Emerson could also find justification in nature for Whitman's alternate bursts of energy and indolence: "Motion or change, and identity or rest, are the first and second secrets of nature: Motion and Rest."[41]

Whitman was always a solitary figure, but never more so than in this crucial period when he was working on *Leaves of Grass*. He was as intimate with his family and yet as remote from them as ever. His brother George's idea of Walt's existence was that "He would lie abed late, and after getting up would write a few hours if he took the notion—perhaps would go off the rest of the day. We were all at work—all except Walt."[42] I am indebted to Mr Charles E. Feinberg for pointing out that, although

this statement was made by George, it was not correct.
Walt's view of it was that he was making good money as
a carpenter until this "*Leaves of Grass* bee came to me." It
forced him to work under "great pressure, pressure from
within."

By the spring of 1855 he was supervising the printing of
the book, setting a few pages himself, at the shop of two
friends of his, the Rome brothers. Somehow or another
he was paying for it himself. He took at few copies home.
George's comment was: "I saw the book—didn't read it
at all—didn't think it worth reading—fingered it a little.
Mother thought as I did—did not know what to make of
it."[43] Nor did anyone else when the book was finally
published on 4 July 1855. Almost no one bought the little
book of 95 pages, with a nine-page essay; it had no name
on the title page, but there was a frontispiece engraving
of Whitman looking much like the engraver's later description of Whitman at this time: "in his red flannel shirt—
minus coat and vest and wore his broad brimmed felt hat
with a rakish kind of slant like the mast of a schooner."[44]

A week later Walt's father died; he had been ill and
paralysed and had not seen any of Walt's work. The poet's
comment was that it would not have made any difference
if he had.

What did make a profound difference was that a copy
of the poems had been sent to Emerson, who not only
read the book immediately but made one of the great
snap judgments of literary history, all the more extraordinary when one considers how oddly those poems
must have shambled into the trim countryside of New
England. The letter is worth quoting in full, for many
reasons.

Concord, Mass^{tts.}
21 July 1855

Dear Sir,

     I am not blind to the worth of the wonderful
gift of "Leaves of Grass." I find it the most extra-

ordinary piece of wit and wisdom that America has yet contributed. I am very happy in reading it, as great power makes us happy. It meets the demand I am always making of what seemed the sterile and stingy nature, as if too much handiwork or too much lymph in the temperament were making our western wits fat and mean. I give you joy of your free and brave thought. I have great joy in it. I find incomparable things said incomparably well, as they must be. I find the courage of treatment, which so delights us, and which large perception only can inspire.

I greet you at the beginning of a great career, which yet must have had a long foreground somewhere, for such a start. I rubbed my eyes a little to see if this sunbeam were no illusion; but the solid sense of the book is a sober certainty. It has the best merits, namely, of fortifying and encouraging.

I did not know until I, last night, saw the book advertised in a newspaper, that I could trust the name as real and available for a post office. I wish to see my benefactor, and have felt much like striking my tasks, and visiting New York to pay you my respects.

R. W. Emerson[45]

Charles A. Dana wrote a sympathetic review in the New York *Tribune*, and a few months later Whitman shamelessly allowed him to publish Emerson's letter. However, Emerson was not very offended, for he visited Whitman at the end of the year. With even less shame, but with more justification from the habits of the age, Whitman wrote various reviews of the book himself. Whittier threw his copy in the fire. Longfellow, Holmes and Lowell kept clear of it. Abraham Lincoln read and enjoyed it, but brought it back to the office with him, remarking that "he had barely saved it from being puri-fied by fire by the women."

The first edition contained the essay and twelve poems,

which were untitled, (they included what are now known as "Song of Myself," "A Song for Occupations," "The Sleepers" and "A Child went forth").

The essay set forth, in the prose of a strong speaking voice, Whitman's beliefs about America and the poet, about nature, simplicity and faith, about the deficiencies of the ordinary, solid, money-making citizen as contrasted with the true object of living, which is to achieve what an earlier English poet called "a wonderfully comprehensive soul." The preface contains what is perhaps the finest of Whitman's many credos:

> This is what you shall do: Love the earth and sun and the animals, despise riches, give alms to everyone that asks, stand up for the stupid and crazy, devote your income and labor to others, hate tyrants, argue not concerning God, have patience and indulgence toward the people, take off your hat to nothing known or unknown, or to any man or number of men—go freely with powerful uneducated persons, and with the young, and with the mothers of families—re-examine all you have been told in school or church or in any book, and dismiss whatever insults your own soul; and your very flesh shall be a great poem, and have the richest fluency, not only in its words, but in the silent lines of its lips and face, and between the lashes of your eyes, and in every motion and joint of your body.[46]

The religious note of this is unmistakable, as is also the typical Whitman mixture of idealism and down-to-earth independence. The poet becomes an intermediary between the poem that he writes and the poem that he or anyone else may become. Even the United States are essentially a poem, the greatest, according to Whitman. This would be intolerable looseness of language, were it not for the fact that for Whitman the parts that go to make up the whole man or nation are essentially the same as those that go to make up the whole poem. The poet is both enormously proud of his calling and responsibilities and capable of endless humility:

There is that indescribable freshness and unconsciousness about an illiterate person, that humbles and mocks the power of the noblest expressive genius. The poet sees for a certainty how one not a great artist may be just as sacred and perfect as the greatest artist.[47]

Whitman's "unconsciousness" is not quite the same as the modern use of the word "unconscious," nevertheless in the period of gestation of *Leaves of Grass* he had managed, in the words of the Keats he had disagreed with, to "absorb the identity of others, and the experience of others," and fuse them with his own dreams and desires to make a new poetic identity of his own, capable of infinite extension and adaptation and yet unmistakably individual. This is the great theme of *Leaves of Grass*, given its most powerful symbolic treatment in "The Sleepers" and fullest treatment in "Song of Myself." It is also this that makes the book so revolutionary and extraordinarily original, with its interior drama, its witty contrasts, its ability to contain both lyric and argument, its ability to hold time in the right hand and space in the left. The "I" of *Leaves of Grass* anticipates such different creations as T. S. Eliot's Tiresias and James Joyce's Bloom, just as the organic wholeness of its conception would have met with Coleridge's approval. It has the same permanently modern quality as any great dramatic figure, although Whitman's "I" has no specific tragedy or comedy to fulfil; it simply exists as comedy, and sometimes tragedy, in the same way as every individual does, and the spontaneous nature of its associations, as the unlimited extent of its sympathies, makes it available to everyone. What Whitman says is true: "I stop somewhere waiting for you."[48]

Another bizarre fact about *Leaves of Grass* is that it was distributed by Fowler and Wells, the phrenologists who had read Whitman's bumps. They also published a weekly magazine called *Life Illustrated*, for which Whitman wrote articles in 1855 and 1856; the magazine also gave publicity to the book and reprinted any favourable reviews, especially one from the London *Dispatch* and a fluttering rave from the popular New York journalist Fanny Fern. Meanwhile Whitman had been working on a second and enlarged edition, which appeared in September 1856; this was in a smaller format, of 384 pages, with Emerson's greeting printed down the backstrip in gold letters. The whole letter was printed in the back, together with a letter from Whitman to Emerson, boldly and untruthfully claiming that the first edition had sold out, and going on to proclaim himself as the great American poet. Thirty-three years later Whitman said to Traubel: "I don't imagine I was guiltless: someone had to speak for me: no one would: I spoke for myself."[49] There is a streak of the charlatan in most writers of genius; Whitman should be forgiven his, especially when one considers how lonely and revolutionary a figure he was.

As for the text of the poems, Whitman had revised those printed in the first edition, and added several more, notably "Sun-down Poem," which was later called "Crossing Brooklyn Ferry."

The more Whitman identified himself as a poet with the life of the United States, the more he worried about the appallingly low level of social and political morality in the country in 1856. Two of his harshest and most deeply felt pieces of writing, if not the best in quality, are the verse "Poem of the Proposition of Nakedness" (later called "Respondez!" and finally rejected) and the prose pamphlet "The Eighteenth Presidency." The verse is sustained irony and sarcastic denunciation, with the message of "let there be apathy under the stars!" The prospect of contemporary America offended against everything that he preached in *Leaves of Grass*.

Let there be money, business, imports, exports, custom, authority, precedents, pallor, dyspepsia, smut, ignorance, unbelief! . . .

Let all the men of These States stand aside for a few smouchers! let the few seize on what they choose! let the rest gawk, giggle, starve, obey![50]

The pamphlet was never published in Whitman's lifetime. Its furious oratory attacked the same enemies as the poem, with more emphasis on political jobbery and the acceptance of slavery. This passionate concern with his country must always offset Whitman's egotism; it is also a creative passion, for which patriotism is too limiting a word, as it rises from a desire to unify the different States and to help form the already distinctive but as yet disorganised American character.

He was sufficiently well-known by now for various eminent visitors to cross the ferry to Brooklyn to see him. Bronson Alcott and Henry Thoreau came, and Alcott wrote in his *Journal* much the best description of the poet in what might be described as Mask Number Two, the dandified editor having long since been put away:

Broad-shouldered, rouge-fleshed, Bacchus-browed, bearded like a satyr, and rank, he wears his man-Bloomer in defiance of everybody, having these as everything else after his own fashion, and for example to all men hereafter. Red flannel undershirt, open-breasted, exposing his brawny neck; striped calico jacket over this, the collar Byroneal, with coarse cloth overalls buttoned to it; cowhide boots; a heavy roundabout, with huge outside pockets and buttons to match; and a slouched hat, for house and street alike. Eyes gray, unimaginative, cautious yet sagacious; his voice deep, sharp, tender sometimes and almost melting. When talking will recline upon the couch at length, pillowing his head upon his bended arm, and informing you naïvely how lazy he is, and slow. Listens well; asks

c

you to repeat what he has failed to catch at once, yet hesitates in speaking often, or gives over as if fearing to come short of the sharp, full, concrete meaning of his thought. Inquisitive, very; over-curious even; inviting criticisms on himself, on his poems—pronouncing it "pomes."—In fine, an egoist, incapable of omitting, or suffering any one long to omit, noting Walt Whitman in discourse. Swaggy in his walk, burying both hands in his outside pockets. Has never been sick, he says, nor taken medicine, nor sinned; and so is quite innocent of repentance and man's fall. A bachelor, he professes great respect for women.[51]

Alcott's description of Whitman's room is also revealing. At this time Mrs Whitman and the family were living with him:

He takes us up two narrow flights of stairs to sit or stand as might in his attic study—also the bed-chamber of himself and his feeble brother (Eddie), the pressure of whose bodies was still apparent in the unmade bed standing in one corner, and the vessel scarcely hidden underneath.[52]

No wonder Walt's "pomes" made such a fetish of health and beauty and freedom!

But despite such visits Whitman was not proving to be the triumphant poet of democracy. The second edition of *Leaves of Grass* was a complete flop, and at the beginning of 1857 he was reduced to borrowing $200 from James Parton, the husband of Fanny Fern. However, he secured another editorship in the spring, this time in the Brooklyn *Daily Times*, and this kept him going financially, despite an unpleasant interlude when Parton sued him for the $200, and Whitman had to hand over books, an oil painting and other goods as payment. He stayed with the *Times* until the middle of 1859, working meanwhile on a new edition of *Leaves of Grass*, which he planned to increase in size from thirty-two to a hundred poems, the additions beings mostly of short length. He had these set in type by his friends the Rome brothers, not for publication but to see them in print, always a further stage in a poem's growth, and make further corrections. The Rome brothers kept Whitman's manuscripts, so it is possible to trace the various stages of his emotional and literary development.

At some stage during these years 1856–60 Whitman passed through a period of doubt and despair, despite the impenetrable mask that led Alcott to think him "quite innocent of repentance and man's fall." The greatest poem composed in this period, "Out of the Cradle," is an acceptance of loneliness, lost love, and death. The long poem "Premonition" (later, "Starting from Paumanok") fights its way to a positive statement from a victory in an inner struggle, a victory that, like so many of Whitman's, is won by being honest about himself, by not being afraid to let the light in on his unconscious desires. In the original version it reads:

I believe the main purport of America is to found a new
    ideal of manly friendship, more ardent, more general,
I will therefore let appear these burning fires that were
    threatening to consume me,
I will lift what has too long kept down those smoulder-
    ing fires—I will now expose and use them.[53]

This does not, however, mean an abandonment to homosexuality, but a typically transcendental vision of a new America buoyed up from its failures by the ideal of comradeship. The ending of the poem (in its final version) is Shelley-like in the pure ardour of its ecstasy.

O camerado close! O you and me at last, and us two
    only.
O a word to clear one's path ahead endlessly!—
O something ecstatic and undemonstrable! O music
    wild!
O now I triumph—and you shall also;

> O hand in hand—O wholesome pleasure—O one more
> desirer and lover!
> O to haste firm holding—to haste, haste on with me.[54]

This is the forward movement characteristic of Whitman's moods of optimism. But this is achieved as a result of having "let appear these burning fires that were threatening to consume me." These fires did not run like a bushfire in a wind, they were within, kept-down, smouldering. Whitman came to terms with them in the "Calamus" poems. In the manuscripts left with the Rome brothers, these poems were first assembled by Whitman into a group of twelve that make a story of a homosexual love-affair. It begins with loneliness, the poem about the live-oak in Louisiana; there is happiness at night on the beach where the waves congratulate him:

> For the friend I love lay sleeping by my side,
> In the stillness his face was inclined towards me, while
> the moon's clear beams shone,
> And his arm lay lightly over my breast—And that night
> I was happy.[55]

But by the eighth poem in the series he is alone and forgotten, harbouring anguish and passion.

> Sullen and suffering hours—(I am ashamed—but it is
> useless—I am what I am;)[56]

At the end of the series he has achieved something of the same generalised passion as at the end of "Starting from Paumanok." In the next edition of *Leaves of Grass* these poems were rearranged amongst the larger group of poems called "Calamus." There is no evidence whether the love-affair was a matter of flesh and blood or of imagination; in either case it was real enough. After all, he said himself that he was the "indirect" poet, and to one of his English admirers confessed: "There is something in my nature *furtive*, like an old hen!"[57] What does seem certain is that under that bland exterior Whitman had come to poetical and emotional terms with his homosexuality and was able to preserve his equilibrium not by repressing it nor by concentrating it on one sensual object, but by diffusing it in "adhesiveness" (a term picked up from phrenology) or the manly love of comrades.

At a different remove from these solitary struggles, Whitman frequently used to visit Pfaff's restaurant on Broadway, where the wits and Bohemians of New York ate, drank, and talked, with Whitman, as might be imagined, remaining slightly apart. One with whom he made friends was Henry Clapp, editor of the *Saturday Press*, who published the first version of "Out of the Cradle endlessly rocking" (called "A Child's Reminiscence") in his Christmas 1859 number. This was a help towards recognition, but a far more exciting encouragement came from Boston in February, with an offer from two publishers, Thayer and Eldridge, to bring out a new edition of *Leaves of Grass*. Whitman was in Boston in March, and almost immediately had a two-hour talk with Emerson, who tried to persuade him not to print the series of poems later called *Children of Adam*; Whitman refused. Nevertheless, Emerson was most genial, even if Mrs Emerson (together with the womenfolk of the other New England writers) refused to have him in the house. The third edition appeared in May, a book of 456 pages; besides much new material, the old work had been revised and rearranged according to Whitman's notions that the book itself ought to have some sort of structure. These and later rearrangements did little but make it difficult for a reader to find his way around the poems. The edition itself received wider attention than any previous one, even though there was a great deal of indignation generated at Whitman's openness about sex, and Whitman was still far from the general acclaim as the bard of America that he so badly needed. Nevertheless, the Boston imprint had extended Whitman's influence, he had made some valuable friends there (such as William Douglas O'Connor), and Lowell had printed "Bardic Symbols" ("As I ebb'd with the Ocean of Life") in the *Atlantic Monthly*.

He returned to Brooklyn and New York and his usual pleasures and pursuits, such as visiting sick omnibus-drivers and firemen in hospital. He was walking down Broadway one night, having been to the opera, when the newsboys came tearing up the street with an extra. It was 13 April 1861, and the news was the firing of the Confederate guns on Fort Sumter. Whitman says:

I bought an extra and cross'd to the Metropolitan hotel (Niblo's) where the great lamps were still brightly blazing, and, with a crowd of others, who gather'd impromptu, read the news, which was evidently authentic. For the benefit of some who had no papers, one of us read the telegram aloud, while all listened silently and attentively. No remark was made by any of the crowd, which had increas'd to thirty or forty, but all stood a minute or two, I remember, before they dispers'd.[58]

Three days later he wrote in his notebook:

I have this day, this hour, resolved to inaugurate for myself a pure, perfect, sweet, clean-blooded robust body, by ignoring all drinks but water and pure milk, and all fat meats, late suppers—a great body, a purged, cleansed, spiritualized, invigorated body.[59]

It sounded as if Whitman was about to make a further identification between himself and the cause of what he called "*the flag*," but it was his brother George who enlisted. As in everything else, Whitman was slow in working out what he was going to do about the War, even though the Battle of Bull Run prompted him to write a popular poem that sounded like a bad newspaper editorial. Besides, Whitman was forty-two; contemporaries like Lowell and Melville did not volunteer.

He continued with journalism, writing articles for the Brooklyn *Standard*, and the hospital that he visited was now taking in many soldiers, with whom he made friends immediately; his first four articles were about this hospital on Broadway. For a year and a half there was no change in the tempo of Whitman's life, and one wonders how much longer his state of inertia would have continued if George, his brother, had not been wounded in December 1862. This had been another of those strange fallow periods, as before the writing of the poems in the first edition of *Leaves of Grass*, when Whitman was in the process of growing another self, to be disguised under another mask. In the polarities of his character, the proud, lonely poet must also be the humble companion of illiterate ferrymen and omnibus-drivers; however, although they enjoyed his company and were no doubt grateful when he looked after the tickets for them, (then as now there were no conductors in New York buses), there could have been no certainty of need on their part. Whitman's desire to be needed comes piercingly through every aspect of his life and poetry. The sprawling "I" of his poems is one that longs to be taken as a lover. He remained devoted to his mother and extraordinarily fond of his odd family, but there was no single human being who could satisfy his complex desires, let alone want him without wanting to possess him. By a typical contradiction, he could only manage an intimate relationship at a distance; the War gave him the great chance of contact between the many and the one which he had called for without ever knowing how to find it.

He left for Washington immediately, taking $50 with him, to find and nurse George. He had his pocket picked in Philadelphia and arrived without a dime, not knowing where to look amongst the dozens of hospitals. Altogether he put in "about three days of the greatest suffering I ever experienced in my life"[60] before he found George in a camp hospital near Fredericksburg, slightly wounded in the cheek. Whitman was used to hospitals, but not such as these, with, ten yards in front of the building, "a heap of amputated feet, legs, arms, etc., a full load for a one-horse cart."[61] He immediately began to visit the wounded, no matter of which side. "I do not see that I do much good to those wounded and dying;" he wrote; "but I cannot leave them. Once in a while some youngster holds on to me convulsively, and I do what I can for him; at any rate, stop with him and sit near him for hours, if he wishes it."[62]

A few days later he returned to Washington. There his friend William O'Connor and his wife found him lodgings in the building where they lived, and his Boston publisher, Eldridge, now assistant to the Army Paymaster, got him work as a copyist in the Paymaster's office. It was not a very exacting job, and left him plenty of time for visiting the hospitals. For the next two years, apart from having to return to Brooklyn owing to family troubles and a breakdown of his own health, Whitman's life alternated between working on odd jobs, as a clerk in government offices, and visiting the wounded. He had assumed the third mask, which William O'Connor was to give the name of "The Good Gray Poet."

It must be emphasised that this hospital visiting was not a sentimental or morbid activity undertaken for want of something more useful. It was an integral element of Whitman's character, and stemmed directly from his New York visits to the sick bus-drivers. He had even prophesied it in "Song of Myself":

Agonies are one of my changes of garments,
I do not ask the wounded person how he feels, I myself
   become the wounded person,
My hurts turn livid upon me as I lean on a cane and
   observe. . . .

I seize the descending man and raise him with resistless
   will,

O despairer, here is my neck,
By God, you shall not go down! hang your whole weight
    upon me.[63]

In a highly-organised modern hospital, let alone in wartime, such private charity would be impossible, but no
one in authority stopped him; and the very fact that his
visits were merely private must have impressed the soldiers, who then as now were suspicious of those coming
from organisations. Whitman's gift of sympathy was not
mawkish nor clinical; he presented himself as an image
of life and health, quite deliberately. He knew it would
not be easy: "One has much to learn to do good in these
places. Great tact is required."[64] He used his small resources to buy things for the soldiers, letter-paper and
envelopes, oranges, tobacco and jellies, but most of all it
was the gift of himself that counted, the gift that he had
always wanted to be able to make, and to know that it
was received. (Of course it should be pointed out, as he
did himself, that he also "bestowed as almoner for others,
many, many, thousands of dollars.")[65] Later, in *Specimen
Days*, he wrote:

In my visits to the hospitals I found it was in the simple
matter of personal presence, and emanating ordinary
cheer and magnetism, that I succeeded and help'd
more than by medical nursing, or delicacies, or gifts of
money, or anything else. During the war I possess'd
the perfection of physical health. My habit, when
practicable, was to prepare for starting out on one of
those daily or nightly tours of from a couple to four or
five hours, by fortifying myself with previous rest, the
bath, clean clothes, a good meal, and as cheerful an
appearance as possible.[66]

He certainly needed that appearance of cheerfulness.
His descriptions, in *Specimen Days* and in his letters, of
the effects of war are some of the most moving ever
written; the suffering had purged Whitman's prose of its

oratorical elements, and the strong emotion remaining comes direct from the event itself. The sensitivity of Whitman's prose adapts itself so well to the public scene or the intimate drama that the quality of it can only be conveyed by extensive quotation. Here is an extract from *Specimen Days*, about a night battle:

Then the camps of the wounded—O heavens, what scene is this?—is this indeed *humanity*—these butcher's shambles? There are several of them. There they lie, in the largest, in an open space in the woods, from 200 to 300 poor fellows—the groans and screams—the odor of blood, mixed with the fresh scent of the night, the grass, the trees—that slaughter-house! O well is it their mothers, their sisters cannot see them—cannot conceive, and never conceiv'd, these things. One man is shot by a shell, both in the arm and leg—both are amputated—there lie the rejected members. Some have their legs blown off—some bullets through the breast— some indescribably horrid wounds in the face or head, all mutilated, sickening, torn, gouged out—some in the abdomen—some mere boys—many rebels, badly hurt —they take their regular turns with the rest, just the same as any—the surgeons use them just the same. Such is the camp of the wounded—such a fragment, a reflection afar off of the bloody scene—while all over the clear, large moon comes out at times softly, quietly shining. Amid the woods, that scene of flitting souls— amid the crack and crash and yelling sounds—the impalpable perfume of the woods—and yet the pungent, stifling smoke—the radiance of the moon, looking from heaven at intervals so placid—the sky so heavenly —the clear obscure up there, those buoyant upper oceans—a few large placid stars beyond, coming silently and languidly out, and then disappearing—the melancholy, draperied night above, around. And there, upon the roads, the fields, and in those woods, that contest,

never one more desperate in any age or land—both
parties now in force—masses—no fancy battle, no
semi-play, but fierce and savage demons fighting there
—courage and scorn of death the rule, exceptions
almost none.[67]

Now the private scene, when those fierce and savage
demons are reduced to men again, very conscious of
death; this is from a letter to his mother, typical in its
directness and simplicity:

One soldier brought here about fifteen days ago, very
low with typhoid fever, Livingston Brooks, Co. B.,
17th Penn. Cavalry, I have particularly stuck to, as I
found him to be in what appeared to be a dying condition, from negligence and a horrible journey of
about forty miles, bad roads and fast driving; and then
after he got here, as he is a simple country boy, very
shy and silent, and made no complaint, they neglected
him. I found him something like I found John Holmes
last winter. I called the doctor's attention to him, shook
up the nurses, had him bathed in spirits, gave him
lumps of ice, and ice to his head; he had a fearful
bursting pain in his head, and his body was like fire.
He was very quiet, a very sensible boy, old fashioned;
he did not want to die, and I had to lie to him without
stint, for he thought I knew everything, and I always
put in of course that what I told him was exactly the
truth, and that if he got really dangerous I would tell
him and not conceal it. The rule is to remove bad
fever patients out from the main wards to a tent by
themselves, and the doctor told me he would have to
be removed. I broke it gently to him, but the poor boy
got it immediately in his head that he was marked with
death, and was to be removed on that account. It had
a great effect upon him, and although I told the truth
this time it did not have as good a result as my former
fibs. I persuaded the doctor to let him remain. For three

days he lay just about an even chance, go or stay, with
a little leaning toward the first. But, mother, to make
a long story short, he is now out of any immediate
danger. He has been perfectly rational throughout—
begins to taste a little food (for a week he ate nothing;
I had to compel him to take a quarter of an orange
now and then), and I will say, whether anyone calls
it pride or not, that if he *does* get up and around again
it's me that saved his life. Mother, as I have said in
former letters, you can have no idea how these sick and
dying youngsters cling to a fellow, and how fascinating
it is, with all its hospital surroundings of sadness and
scenes of repulsion and death.[68]

Note Whitman's honesty here. He used the word
"fascination" in other letters to describe his reaction to
the hospitals. And in a letter to one of his New York
cronies, companions at Pfaff's and the opera, sharers of
rambles through the Bowery, he says: "I will confess to
you dear Hugo that in some respects I find myself in my
element amid these scenes."[69]

Two things emerge from this. Firstly, Whitman always
made the clearest and most positive distinction between
sickness and health, between the vigorous and the morbid, yet no one was more conscious than he of the inter-
changes electrically moving between those two opposite
poles. He was the man, "220 pounds avoirdupois ... a
regular model,"[70] who came home across Brooklyn ferry
to sleep in the same bed as his crippled, idiot brother.
His "fascination" with the wounds and dysentery and
fever came from his dramatic sense that health might be
restored and himself be the agent.

Secondly, the homosexual comradeship that he longed
for was kept in a context of present need, however pathet-
ically some of Whitman's passionate letters to Lewy
Brown or Tom Sawyer reveal the hope that the relationship should continue after the War. Once again, Whit-

man was fortunate in living in the pre-Freudian age. The emotion pours out of him as an extraordinary mixture that no worried analysis has turned sour. One moment he is a lover, another a father, another a comrade. The marvel is that a man so self-conscious could be so little in danger of a sterile self-obsession, that one so knowledgeable about himself could remain so innocent. The full complexity, and yet the utter simplicity, of Whitman's situation comes through unadorned in a letter to a woman in Boston asking for aid for the soldiers in hospital:

I have long discarded all stiff conventions (they and I are too near to each other, there is no time to lose, and death and anguish dissipate ceremony here between my lads and me)—I pet them, some of them it does so much good, they are so faint and lonesome—at parting at night sometimes I kiss them right and left—The doctors tell me I supply the patients with a medicine which all their drugs and bottles and powders are helpless to yield.[71]

The latter claim is amply borne out by the testimony of various doctors.

During 1863 Whitman continued to see a great deal of the O'Connors, and he made a most important new friend in John Burroughs. The news from his family was getting worse and worse. Money was as short as ever; Jesse was growing sicker and nearer to violent insanity; Andrew was drunk most of the time, dying of tuberculosis of the throat; there was a possibility that Jeff, the only one with a job, would be drafted. Walt made a quick trip home in November, and did what he could to cheer up his mother. In a letter written to his ex-publisher Eldridge at this time there is a significant passage about her:

The great recompense of my journey here is to see my mother so well, & so bravely sailing on amid many discouragements like a noble old ship—. . . Charley I

think sometimes to be a woman is greater than to be a
man—is more eligible to greatness, not the ostensible
article, but the real one.[72]

The same letter also has an important reference to
Whitman's feeling at this time about his situation as a
writer. He had another volume of verse ready for publication, *Drum-Taps*, and was impatient to find some means
of bringing it out. "I *must*," he writes, "be continually
bringing out poems—now is the hey day—I shall range
along the high plateau of my life and capacity for a few
years now, & then swiftly descend." It is obvious that the
enormous energy he had put into his activities as a
hospital visitor had in no sense drained off his poetic
resources.

Back in Washington, Whitman, assisted by his friends,
was still trying to find permanent employment as a clerk
with the Government. Unfortunately, his reputation as
the author of *Leaves of Grass*, that notorious book, stood
in his way. He was living in extreme simplicity, in a
garret, spending some time listening (rather disillusioned)
to Congress, hoping to make some money out of lectures
or the publication of *Drum-Taps*. By June he was con-
fessing to his mother: "I do not feel as first rate as usual.
. . . I believe I am homesick—something new for me—
then I have seen all the horrors of soldiers' life and not
been kept up by its excitement."[73] Soon he was having
"spells of deathly faintness and bad trouble in my head
too, and sore throat (quite a little budget, ain't they?)"[74]
By the end of June he was back in Brooklyn and in a
couple of months his health had recovered. He stayed
there for six months, although he was eager to get to
Washington; the chance came in January 1865, when,
thanks to O'Connor's efforts, he was appointed as a clerk
in the Indian Bureau of the Department of the Interior,
at $1,200 a year. It was an easy job which suited him
very well, and for the moment his only worries were

about his brother George, who had been taken prisoner; he was, however, safe, and was released in February. He took pleasant walks in the woods with his friend Burroughs, who was a naturalist and told him amongst other things about the song of the hermit thrush, later to be such a vital symbol in Whitman's great elegy for Lincoln. Whitman was at home on leave when the news came through of the murder of the President. "Mother," he wrote, "prepared breakfast—and other meals afterwards—as usual; but not a mouthful was eaten all day by either of us. We each drank half a cup of coffee; that was all. Little was said. We got every newspaper morning and evening, and the frequent extras of that period, and pass'd them silently to each other."[75]

At last, in May 1865, *Drum-Taps* was printed. This was a book of poems on a national subject, containing no awkward material about sex, and Whitman thought it would at last establish him as the national poet. Actually not all the poems were on war subjects, and after the first few copies the book was bound with *Sequel to Drum-Taps*, which contained the Lincoln elegy. There was no immediate impact and it was some time before any reviews appeared. Meanwhile, out of the blue, Whitman received an official notice telling him he was fired from his job. His friends were as indignant as Walt was stupefied; it appeared that the new Secretary of the Interior, Harlan, had found or been shown the annotated copy of *Leaves of Grass* on Whitman's desk, and decided that Whitman was an immoral character. Fortunately Ashton, the Assistant Attorney General, persuaded Harlan not to oppose Whitman's transfer to the Attorney General's Department, and Whitman was back in a job again.

By November, reviews of *Drum-Taps* were appearing, and they were not very encouraging; the most ferocious was an anomymous one in the *Nation*, written by a young man of twenty-two, Henry James. In January, these setbacks were, however, more than counter-balanced by the publication of William O'Connor's monograph *The Good Gray Poet* which attacked Harlan and the whole principle of literary censorship, and eulogised Whitman almost into a sort of Christ-figure. Whitman had created this mask for himself; now someone had given it a name.

Almost equally important to Whitman's emotional life was his meeting, in an "awful storm," with an eighteen-year-old Virginian horse-car conductor, Peter Doyle; Whitman formed a passionate friendship with him which operated, more than any previous relationship, on a father-son basis. Unlike wartime friends such as Tom Sawyer, Doyle remained devoted to Whitman for many years.

In August 1867 Whitman obtained leave and went to New York to supervise the printing of the fourth edition of *Leaves of Grass*—"that unkillable work!" as he put it[76]—which contained revisions and rearrangements of the earlier poems, plus *Drum-Taps* and its *Sequel*. Despite the cool reception of *Drum-Taps*, Whitman was cheerful and confident, and by now he had good friends to support him; when the book appeared, the New York *Times* gave a huge amount of space to a review by O'Connor, and on its own account added (even though it considered the book "too indecent to be circulated freely") some favourable editorial comments. Further important developments were taking place in England, where the *Fortnightly Review* had published a very favourable review written by Moncure Conway, who had visited Whitman in Brooklyn in 1855. (Whitman was peeved with some of the biographical details, which were indeed a bit steep, particularly the anecdote of Conway finding Whitman lying on the sand, with the thermometer at 100 degrees; Conway alleged that he asked Whitman if he was not bothered by the heat, to which Whitman answered, not at all, it was "one of his favourite places and attitudes for composing 'pomes'.")

Whitman was often to be upset, hardly with reason, when one of his masks was used to create a myth.

In July 1867, William Rossetti wrote a panegyric of Whitman in the London *Chronicle*, and after various instructions and counter-instructions from Whitman about possible expurgations, Rossetti edited a volume of selections which was published in February 1868. The influence that this volume exercised, and the importance of the English writers who championed Whitman as a result of it, established the basis of his international fame. He was now a poet of the English language, not only the (mostly rejected) American bard.

Also at this time a new magazine, *Galaxy*, gave him space for long prose essays, and he had his chance to castigate the post-War nation and suggest remedies in "Democracy" and "Personalism." Distinguished visitors called on him in Washington, Swinburne praised him in England; the old stalwarts of New England mostly, however, continued to oppose him, although the *Atlantic* printed a long poem of his in February 1869. The only thing that was constantly bad was the money-troubles of his family, and squabbles between Mrs Whitman and Jeff and his wife. Yet there were ominous cracks in the magnificent frame of the poet of perfect health; in the summer of 1869 he complained frequently of dizzy spells and sudden sweats.

In March 1870, Jesse died in a lunatic asylum; it is worth quoting Mrs Whitman's letter to Walt on hearing the news to give an indication of her good-hearted simplicity:

o Walt aint it sad to think the poor soul hadent a friend near him in his last moments   and to think he had a paupers grave   i know it makes no difference but if he could have been buried decently. . . . i was thinking of him more lately than common   i wish Walter you would write to Jeff and hanna that

D

he is dead   i will write to george   i feel very sad of course Walt if he has done ever so wrong he was my **first born**   but gods will be done   good bie Walter dear[77]

There is no doubt that Whitman's life-long respect for the simple and the ill-educated came from his love for his mother.

All those who knew Whitman at this time remarked on his extraordinary personality and magnificent appearance, which were lent a peculiar magnetism by his sense of dignity and calm, his sincerity and candour. Yet his notebooks reveal that those torments of earlier years were visiting him as strongly as ever before. The exact nature of the emotion is baffling, even if the strength of it is obvious:

cheating, childish abandonment of myself, fancying what does not really exist in another, but is all the time in myself alone—utterly deluded & cheated by *myself*, & my own weakness—REMEMBER WHERE I AM MOST WEAK, & most lacking. Yet always preserve a kind spirit & demeanor to 16. But PURSUE HER NO MORE.

It is IMPERATIVE, that I obviate & remove myself (& **my** orbit) *at all hazards* from this *incessant enormous* & PERTURBATION

TO GIVE UP ABSOLUTELY & *for good, from this present hour*, this FEVERISH, FLUCTUATING, *useless undignified pursuit of 164—too long*, (*much too long*) persevered in,— so humiliating—*It must come at last* & had better come now—(*It cannot possibly be a success*) LET THERE FROM THIS HOUR BE NO FALTERING, NO GETTING—*at all henceforth*, (NOT ONCE, *under any circumstances*)—*avoid seeing her, or meeting her, or any talk or explanations*—or ANY MEETING WHATEVER, FROM THIS HOUR FORTH, FOR LIFE.

Depress the adhesive nature   It is in excess—

making life a torment   All this diseased, feverish
disproportionate *adhesiveness*.[78]

There is not the faintest evidence either from Whitman
or from the testimony of any of his friends that he was
pursuing a woman at this or any other time. It is possible
the old fox wrote "her" for "him," as he had done in one
of his poems, to put readers off the scent. "Adhesiveness"
is his favourite word, taken from phrenological jargon,
for "manly love." Eleven days after making this entry
in his notebook, he left Washington on a trip to Brooklyn,
and a few days later he wrote to Pete Doyle about their
parting that night:

> Pete there was something in that hour from 10 to 11
> o'clock (parting though it was) that has left me pleas-
> ure and comfort for good—I never dreamed that you
> made so much of having me with you, nor that you
> could feel so downcast at losing me. I foolishly thought
> it was all on the other side.[79]

Perhaps, even though he had known Pete for more than
three years, his natural slowness had only just allowed
him to reach the point of knowing that his affection was
returned. Perhaps it was a struggle in which Whitman
was trying to feel like a father and actually feeling like a
lover; it has already been noted how shocked Whitman
was when Symonds tried to force this homosexual passion
out into the open, or rather tried to make, in Whitman's
eyes, a perversion out of an ideal. For Whitman this was
no personal affair, but the basis of new hopes for the
future of his country. Just how seriously he took it can be
gauged from a passage in his long prose work published
in 1871, *Democratic Vistas*. (This was made up of two
published essays, "Democracy" and "Personalism," and
a third unpublished one, "Literature.") In this Whitman
announced that "the personal and passionate attach-
ment of man to man—which, hard to define, underlies
the lessons and ideals of the profound saviours of every

land and age" promises "the most substantial hope and safety of the future of these States." He explained his conviction in a long note:

It is to the development, identification, and general prevalence of that fervid comradeship (the adhesive love, at least rivalling the amative love hitherto possessing imaginative literature, if not going beyond it) that I look for the counterbalance and offset of our materialistic and vulgar American democracy, and for the spiritualization thereof. Many will say it is a dream, and will not follow my inferences: but I confidently expect a time when there will be seen, running like a half-hid warp through all the myriad audible and visible worldly interests of America, threads of manly friendship, fond and loving, pure and sweet, strong and life-long, carried to degrees hitherto unknown—not only giving tone to individual character, and making it unprecedently emotional, muscular, heroic, and refined, but having the deepest relations to general politics. I say democracy infers such loving comradeship, as its most inevitable twin or counterpart, without which it will be incomplete, in vain, and incapable of perpetuating itself.[80]

This is perhaps the deepest and clearest expression of Whitman's idealism; the strains of doubt and sadness in his work spring from his knowledge of its unattainability.

Whitman spent the summer of 1870 in Brooklyn arranging for the printing of a fifth edition of *Leaves of Grass*, and of a new collection, *Passage to India*, of which the title poem had been prompted by the engineering feats of the Suez Canal, the trans-Atlantic cable, and the railway from the Atlantic to the Pacific. Whitman saw in these triumphs proof that God intended that at last the world should attain unity and harmony; he was in an optimistic mood. The new poems, and *Democratic Vistas*, did not cause much of a stir in America; however, in

England Swinburne addressed an ode to him in *Songs before Sunrise*, and a more urgent if embarrassing tribute came in a series of love-letters from Anne Gilchrist. She was a woman of distinguished intellect, widow of Alexander Gilchrist, biographer of William Blake. From the first she had been an ardent admirer of Whitman's poems; Walt had innocently sent her his photograph and instructed Rossetti to show her an appreciative letter. In no time she was offering to come to America and be the mother of his children; Whitman nervously replied that the relation between them was already beautiful and delicate. After more letters from her he hardened his tone slightly, and finally protested that she was constructing "an unauthorized and imaginary figure." At this she abandoned the pursuit, temporarily, although they continued to keep in touch with each other.

Democratic Vistas and the Preface to the 1855 edition of *Leaves of Grass* are Whitman's major essays; one grew naturally out of the ideas of the other. Despite the often breathless prose, *Democratic Vistas* is a powerful expression of Whitman's hates, loves, and hopes. It is also profoundly American in its mixture of pragmatism and idealism, its determination that "ideas of the unknown and of unreality" must fearlessly be brought forward "to confront the growing excess and arrogance of realism."[81] Despite his enthusiasm, Whitman was under no illusions about democracy. "It is useless to deny it: Democracy grows rankly up the thickest, noxious, deadliest plants and fruits of all—brings worse and worse invaders—needs newer, larger, stronger, keener compensations and compellers."[82] Most of what he says is as relevant to democracies today as a hundred years ago, particularly to America itself. His most fervent hope is that imaginative literature will provide what he calls "archetypes" for the future democratic character, that the poet will in fact go a step beyond Shelley's unacknowledged legislator, and that his poetry will "inspire itself with science and the modern,"[83] and unify the country, bringing people into touch with the "idea of All, with the accompanying idea of eternity,"[84] until, strange but typical of Whitman, democracy will produce "great poems of death,"[85] of death as the pulse of re-birth. It is vague, of course, but at least it is not mean or niggling.

Democratic Vistas is also important as a collection of Whitman's ideas on subjects that were vital to him: nature, language, sex, and the whole problem of identity.

In 1872, Whitman's health deteriorated further, and he was deeply shocked by a quarrel with his old friend O'Connor over the voting rights of negroes, a quarrel so violent that O'Connor refused to see him again. Another blow was a hostile criticism of Swinburne's, prompted by Robert Buchanan's celebrated attack on Swinburne and D. G. Rossetti, *The Fleshly School of Poetry*, in which Whitman's old admirer expressed his disgust with the doctrine that was tending to push out the genuine poetry in Whitman's later work. He was indeed, as he had foreseen, descending from the high plateau.

Then, in January 1873, he suffered a stroke which paralysed his left arm and leg. His friends (except O'Connor) rallied round him, and he thought he would soon be over it. But his misfortunes thickened. In February Jeff's wife died, which "much depressed" him. In May he got a message from George, with whom Mrs Whitman was living in Camden, to say that their mother was dying. Whitman managed to get there three days before her death; afterwards, he wrote to Pete Doyle: "It is the great cloud of my life."[86] Whitman had not intended to stay in Camden, but in 1874 he was still there, writing odd pieces of journalism, crossing the river to Philadelphia, and, as usual, enjoying the company of ferrymen, and most importantly, still writing poetry. "Song of the Redwood Tree" and "Prayer of Columbus" were published in *Harper's*; the very fine "Prayer," of a "batter'd, wreck'd old man . . . | Old, poor, and paralysed," he admitted to have "a sort of autobiographical dash in it." Lonely, sick and poor, he brooded more and more on the fact that no American publisher would touch his books, and many bookshops would not handle them, that he was omitted from Emerson's anthology *Parnassus*, and that there were frequent attacks on him in the American press. He probably wrote himself a long article, "Walt Whitman's actual American Position," that appeared in the *West Jersey Press*.[87] He certainly sent a copy to William Rossetti, who immediately, with Robert Buchanan, set about launching an appeal to help Whitman. Some of the old charlatanism was at work here, for his old acquaintance Frank Sanborn visited him at this time and found him living "comfortably and pleasantly, as an invalid can, with his brother, Col. George W. Whitman, who is inspector of gas-pipes in the city of Camden."[88] In England subscribers to his Centennial Edition, many of them paying more than the required ten dollars, included Tennyson, Edmund Gosse, the Rossettis, George Saintsbury, Lord Houghton, and many other names that made even the New York *Tribune* sit up and take notice. This raised Whitman's spirits immensely, and he also found great solace in periods spent at a farm nearby, where his health improved considerably. Mrs Stafford, the farmer's wife, and her family all liked Whitman, and helped him down the hill to Timber Creek until he could hobble there on his own, to swim and sunbathe. He always took a notebook with him, and some of his freshest and most delightful prose comes from the hours of close observation of nature at Timber Creek. There is a charming innocence, none the less so for being slightly comical, in the picture of the sick poet sunning his way back to health:

An hour or so after breakfast I wended my way down to the recesses of the aforesaid dell, which I and certain thrushes, cat-birds, etc., had all to ourselves. A light south-west wind was blowing through the tree-tops. It was just the place and time for my Adamic air-bath and flesh-brushing from head to foot. So hanging my clothes on a rail near by, keeping old broadbrim straw on head and easy shoes on feet, havn't I had a good time the last two hours! First with the stiff-elastic bristles rasping arms, breast, sides, till they turn'd scarlet—then partially bathing in the clear waters of the running brook—taking everything very leisurely, with many rests and pauses—stepping about barefooted every few minutes now and then in some neighbouring black ooze, for unctuous mud-bath to my feet—a brief second and third rinsing in the crystal running waters —rubbing with the fragrant towel—slow negligent promenades on the turf up and down in the sun, varied with occasional rests, and further frictions of the bristle-brush—sometimes carrying my portable chair with me from place to place, as my range is quite extensive here, nearly a hundred rods, feeling quite secure from intrusion, (and that indeed I am not at all nervous about, if it accidentally happens.)

As I walked slowly over the grass, the sun shone out enough to show the shadow moving with me. Somehow I seem'd to get identity with each and every thing around me, in its condition. Nature was naked, and I was also.[89]

Into this paradise, or at least into neighbouring Philadelphia, Mrs Gilchrist irrupted with her children, determined to look after the lonely poet. Actually they all got on very well, without any alarming intimacies, and Whitman frequently used to visit their house, although he was furiously angry when Mrs Gilchrist once visited Timber Creek. Mrs Gilchrist's daughter gives an excellent description of Whitman at this time:

Walt Whitman was at this time fifty-eight, but he

looked seventy. His beard and hair were snow-white, his complexion a fine colour, and unwrinkled. He had still, though stricken in 1873 by paralysis, a most majestic presence. He was over six feet, but he walked lame, and leaning heavily on a stick. He was dressed always in a complete suit of grey clothes with a large spotless white linen collar, the flowing beard filling in the gap at his sunburnt throat.[90]

He had successfully adapted himself to the last of his masks, "The Sage of Camden."

He began to gather disciples around him, such as the young Englishman Edward Carpenter, and the Canadian doctor, R. M. Bucke; he also lost one, in physical proximity if not in devotion, for Mrs Gilchrist moved to Boston. In 1879 he delivered the first of his Lincoln Lectures in Steck Hall in New York, and in the autumn he received a very American-sounding invitation, to be guest of honour and visiting poet at the Kansas Quarter Centennial Celebration in Lawrence, Kansas. At last he had his chance to see the West he had often vicariously visited in his poems; he was also able to see his brother Jeff in St Louis. He went on to Denver, down to Pueblo and home, thrilled by it all, but utterly exhausted as well. Like a true American traveller, he said of the West: "Even their simplest statistics are sublime."

In 1880, he set out again, this time to visit Dr Bucke in London, Ontario; and, in the next year, he was very pleased to be asked to give his Lincoln Lecture in Boston. This now became the rhythm of his life, a more public one than it had ever been before, trips to other states, returning to Camden, revisiting Long Island and the cemeteries where his ancestors were buried. At last an American publisher, and a distinguished one, James Osgood, offered to bring out *Leaves of Grass*. Whitman gave him "fair warning on one point, the sexuality odes about which the original row was started and kept up so long are all retained and must go in the same as ever."[91] Fair warning indeed, for in March 1882—after Whitman had spent some pleasant weeks in August 1881 in Boston seeing it through the press, and after the book had been published and well reviewed, and was selling—the District Attorney of Boston classified *Leaves of Grass* as obscene literature. The poems most objected to, astonishingly enough, were "A Woman waits for Me" and "Ode to a Common Prostitute." Osgood withdrew from publication and handed over the sheets and plates to Whitman in exchange for his royalties. In the subsequent rumpus, Whitman was, for once, supported by most American editors, and his old but estranged friend William O'Connor rallied round him again.

This issue, later published in Philadelphia as the ninth edition, incorporated Whitman's revisions, which attempted to make the book itself the shape of the poet's life, from "One's-self I sing" to "So Long!" He felt at last that the book had "really been published."

In January 1882 Oscar Wilde came to see him and thought him a "grand old man," while Whitman reciprocated by considering Wilde "a great big, splendid boy." Friends came across the river to see him, but Philadelphia society approved neither of him nor his book. In 1884 he bought a house in Mickle Street, Camden, a small wooden affair close to the roar of the railway trucks and well within range of the stink of a fertiliser-factory across the river, where, of course, his beloved ferries were always available to him. He had been able to buy it with $1,250 from royalties on the Philadelphia publication of *Leaves of Grass* and on the volume of prose recollections, *Specimen Days*, with another $500 borrowed from a friend. It must have been a novel sensation for Whitman, first to have made some money from his books, and secondly to be the owner of property; however, the money soon trickled out, and the property was a meagre one. His life grew quieter and quieter; a housekeeper,

Mrs Davis, moved in, an act of some courage when Whitman's notorious reputation is considered. Edmund Gosse called, and left a beautiful description of the old poet, who reminded him of "a great old grey Angora Tom"

clean in the highest degree, raised to the nth power of stainlessness, scoured and scrubbed to such a pitch that dirt seemed defined for all remaining time. Whitman, in particular, in his suit of hodden grey and shirt thrown wide open at the throat, his grey hair and whiter beard voluminously flowing, seemed positively blanched with cleanliness; the whole man sand-white with spotlessness, like a deal table that has grown old under the scrubbing-brush.[92]

Hearing of his worsening lameness, some of his friends asked a selection of well-known people if they would each give ten dollars to buy Whitman a horse and buggy; men like Mark Twain, Holmes, Whittier, and Edwin Booth subscribed immediately, and for the next three years, until 1888, Whitman had a vast amount of pleasure from driving around in his buggy. Rossetti had also been collecting money for him in England, and a fund was promoted in the *Pall Mall Gazette*; the news of a famous but indigent American poet being supported with money raised in England was thoroughly galling to Americans. Andrew Carnegie wrote out a cheque for $350 when Whitman gave his Lincoln Lecture in New York in 1887. Friends in Boston raised $800. Whitman was at least being allowed to die in some dignity. Nor would his appearance be forgotten; painters, sculptors and photographers flocked to Camden to work on him.

In 1888 he had a collapse, and the group of friends who were looking after him secured a nurse, and Horace Traubel, a young disciple, spent a great deal of time with him, indefatigably writing down every word the old poet said, and often needling and teasing him to squeeze a few more words out of him. One feels sorry for Whitman, who never had a private moment when Traubel was around; moreover, Traubel recorded a prodigious amount of rubbish. Nevertheless, Whitman was fond of the young man and there is no doubt that Traubel did more than anyone else to help Whitman in his last years. In 1888, with Traubel's help, he finished work on a volume of prose and poetry, *November Boughs*, which McKay published in Philadelphia in November. The book contains a preface, "A Backward Glance o'er Travel'd Roads," which sums up and says again all that he had been trying to do in *Leaves of Grass*, and in his old age he perceived a profound truth in the relation between his book and the country: "I consider *Leaves of Grass* and its theory experimental—as, in the deepest sense, I consider our American republic itself to be, with its theory."[93] This is what makes the book and the history of nineteenth-century America so exciting, the very act of creation is unfolding before your eyes, with all its freshness, its awkwardness, and its attendant pain.

November Boughs contains a collection of poems called *Sands at Seventy*, the ending of one of which is the best summing-up of Whitman in the final years of his life:

> Soon to be lost for aye in the darkness—loth, O so loth
>   to depart!
> Garrulous to the very last.[94]

In 1890 Whitman gave his Lincoln Lecture in Philadelphia, and later that year Colonel Robert Ingersoll, the famous orator (and, painful to many Philadelphians, agnostic) gave a benefit lecture for Whitman which brought in $870. Less happily for Whitman, his favourite brother Jeff died at the end of November in the same year.

In 1891 he published a last little collection of prose and verse, *Good-bye my Fancy*, and a final edition of *Leaves of Grass* came out in 1892. American to the end, he quietly went out to Harleigh Cemetery, selected a lot, and signed a contract for the building of a huge mausoleum in which all his family, or as many as possible, should be buried with him. This would have cost several thousand dollars, if one of his friends, Harned, had not heard about it and cut the contractor down; as it was, Whitman paid the $1,500 of the original contract.

He died on 26 March 1892. A post-mortem was performed, and the report of the five doctors present stated that it was marvellous that Whitman had survived so long. "It was no doubt due largely to that indomitable will pertaining to Walt Whitman. Another would have died much earlier with one half of the pathological changes which existed in his body."[95] This coexistence of death and life is typical of all Whitman's thinking. "Birth, copulation, and death"; the words have sounded like a drab dirge in the twentieth century. To Whitman they could not be considered apart, and their meaning was joyful. Despite the many, baffling, and deliberate contradictions in his personality, his convictions about birth, sex and death never changed from those stated in the poem written thirty-two years before his death, and which he used as an epilogue for several editions of *Leaves of Grass*.

> Camerado, this is no book,
> Who touches this touches a man. . . .
> Remember my words, I may again return,
> I love you, I depart from materials,
> I am as one disembodied, triumphant, dead.[96]

REFERENCES

1. *W.W.C.*, IV. 121.
2. Pref., *Leaves of Grass* (1855). *C.W.*, v. 182.
3. *W.W.C.*, IV. 87.
4. "A Clear Midnight." *C.W.*, II. 270.
5. "Song of Myself." *C.W.*, I. 80, 81.
6. "Song of Myself." *C.W.*, I. 72.
7. "Song of Myself." *C.W.*, I. 40.

8. *Specimen Days. C.W.*, IV. 10.

9. *Specimen Days. C.W.*, IV. 28.

10. *Specimen Days. C.W.*, IV. 14.

11. *Specimen Days. C.W.*, IV. 16.

12. *Specimen Days. C.W.*, IV. 17.

13. *W.W.C.*, IV. 67.

14. *Specimen Days. C.W.*, IV. 20.

15. *Collect. C.W.*, VI. 5–15.

16. *U.P.P.*, I. 68–9.

17. *W.W.C.*, I. 93.

18. Quoted in *S.S.*, p. 48.

19. Brooklyn *Eagle*, 23 May 1846.

20. Brooklyn *Eagle*, 28 Jul. 1846.

21. *Specimen Days. C.W.*, IV. 24.

22. *The Gathering of the Forces*, edd. C. Rodgers and J. Black, New York and London 1920, VOL. II, pp. 268, 269.

23. *Specimen Days. C.W.*, V. 35.

24. Quoted in Richard V. Chase, *Walt Whitman Reconsidered*, N.Y. and London 1955, pp. 37–8.

25. *U.P.P.*, I. 191.

26. *Complete Poetry and Selected Prose and Letters*, ed. Emory Holloway, London 1938, p. 1052.

27. *W.W.C.*, IV. 312–14.

28. *C.W.*, I. 152–3.

29. *C.W.*, I. 219.

30. Pref., *Leaves of Grass* (1855). *C.W.*, V. 166.

31. This reference cannot now be traced.

32. Emory Holloway, "More Light on Whitman," in *American Mercury*, I (Feb. 1924), p. 184.

33. "Calamus." *C.W.*, I. 141.

34. *C.W.*, IX. 134.

35. *S.S.*, 131.

36. *U.P.P.*, II. 85.

37. *U.P.P.*, II. 72.

38. J. T. Trowbridge, *My Own Story*, Boston 1903, p. 367.

39. R. W. Emerson, *Essays*, Everyman edn., London 1906, pp. 33, 36, 37, 43.

40. *Op. cit.*, p. 302.

41. *Op. cit.*, p. 300.

42. *In Re Walt Whitman*, edd. his literary executors, Philadelphia 1893, p. 35.

43. *In Re Walt Whitman*, p. 35.

44. Quoted in *S.S.*, p. 150.

45. *C.W.*, X. 106.

46. *C.W.*, V. 166–7.

47. *C.W.*, V. 164.

48. "Song of Myself," §52. *C.W.*, I. 109.

49. *W.W.C.*, IV. 152.

50. *C.W.*, III. 313, 314.

51. *The Journals of Bronson Alcott*, ed. Odell Shepard, Boston 1938, pp. 286–7.

52. *Op. cit.*, p. 289.

53. *S.S.*, p. 221.

54. *C.W.*, I. 32.

55. *S.S.*, p. 223.

56. *Op. cit.*, p. 225.

57. E. Carpenter, *Days with Walt Whitman*, London 1906, p. 43.

58. *Specimen Days. C.W.*, IV. 29.

59. H. B. Binns, *A Life of Walt Whitman*, London 1905, p. 181.

60. *C.W.*, VII. 128.

61. *Specimen Days. C.W.*, IV. 38.

62. *Specimen Days. C.W.*, IV. 39.

63. "Song of Myself." *C.W.*, I. 81, 90.

64. *C.W.*, VII. 81–2.

65. *Specimen Days. C.W.*, IV. 97.

66. *Specimen Days. C.W.*, IV. 62.

67. *Specimen Days. C.W.*, IV. 55–56.

78. *C.W.*, VII. 169–70.
79. *Complete Poetry and Selected Prose and Letters*, ed. Holloway, p. 924.
80. *Op. cit.*, p. 898.
81. *W.W.C.*, II. 127.
82. *S.S.*, p. 305.
83. *C.W.*, VII. 273.
84. *C.W.*, VII. 274.
85. *Specimen Days. C.W.*, IV. 37–38.
86. *S.S.*, p. 371.
87. *S.S.*, p. 419.
88. *U.P.P.*, II. 95–6.
89. *C.W.*, VIII. 48.
90. *C.W.*, V. 131.
81. *C.W.*, V. 137.
82. *C.W.*, V. 143.
83. *C.W.*, V. 139.
84. *C.W.*, V. 140.
85. *C.W.*, V. 141.

86. *C.W.*, VIII. 99.
87. *Walt Whitman's Workshop*, ed. C. J. Furness, Cambridge, Mass., 1928, pp. 245–6.
88. *S.S.*, p. 471.
89. *Specimen Days. C.W.*, IV. 183–184.
90. Grace Gilchrist, "Chats with Walt Whitman," in *Temple Bar Magazine*, CXIII (Feb. 1898), pp. 200–12.
91. *C.W.*, VIII. 276.
92. Edmund Gosse, *Critical Kit-Kats*, London and New York 1896, pp. 102, 103.
93. *C.W.*, III. 43.
94. *C.W.*, II. 323.
95. *In Re Walt Whitman*, p. 409.
96. "So Long." *C.W.*, II. 289, 290.

CHAPTER II

THE POETRY

app. to mean man

Any discussion of Whitman as a man must end with his
conviction that his book was himself. But one must be
very wary of beginning any discussion of his poetry with
the assumption that one can believe him when he claims
"I celebrate myself."[1] One should treat it rather as a
vast experiment in becoming. The "myself" breaks down
into many different selves, as the man himself wore
different masks, selves searching out their true relation-
ships with life and death, time and space, nature and the
inhabitants of a democracy, sex and language. Despite
his magnificent gift for creating an unforgettable scene,
for being in a particular place at a particular time, it
always turns out that Whitman has slipped away and is
already somewhere else. His gift of sympathy draws
emotion toward the object, not toward Whitman. Despite those pages of confessions, his secrets are never told.
Only in his bad poems is he unmistakably there, and
then only as a wraith of himself, the newspaper editor
and orator thumping away at his clichés. He is more
akin to Shakespeare than to those who celebrate themselves, like Donne or Yeats. We know exactly how
deliciously Donne's roving hand moved over the naked
body of his mistress, with what a horrible delight Yeats
found himself a randy old man. But Whitman, like
Shakespeare, is "Both in and out of the game and
watching and wondering at it," and one of his most
remarkable qualities is that without projecting himself
into dramatic characters with a life of their own he
manages to populate *Leaves of Grass* with a personality that

is at once myriad and unmistakably individual. It is partly this fluidity of Whitman's that enables him to seep through all barriers; at his best he does not date at all. It is also partly that this fluidity is exactly and purely conveyed in his language. Whitman exemplifies all that this age has been retaught about the relation between poetry and "language such as men do use," even if some of the teachers have denied Whitman considerably more than thrice.

One should attempt to consider together Whitman's use of his identity and his use of language; they are elusive, but inseparable. Whitman inherited all the nineteenth-century muddle about art and nature, and gave it a good extra stir himself. Two of his favourite contradictory identities are the bard whose poems bud "as unerringly and loosely as lilacs and roses on a bush," like Keats with his spontaneity of leaves on a tree, and the poet whose notebooks are crammed, whose life is spent in revising and rearranging his poems, and whose conception of his calling is so lofty that he thinks a poet can shape the character of his country. Whitman lived happily with both of these identities, to the fury of those who think that one should plump for the real *or* for the ideal. His life depended on his ability to absorb both, and in embracing such disparate experience Whitman never gives the impression of acting, of indulging in false emotion. Henry Fielding's robust judgment that the true source of the ridiculous is affectation spares Whitman, who was frequently ridiculous, but through *naïveté*, not affectation. His hours of companionship with bus-drivers and ferrymen cannot be construed as an intellectual's slumming, as the idealist indulging in a burst of *nostalgie de la boue*. Nor can his rhapsodies or ardent statements of belief be taken as the sentimental maunderings of a good honest worker after he has had a couple of pints. Whitman lives his way into both identities, with the body and soul that he insisted were indissoluble. Although his

E

critical thinking is as easily punctured as that of Keats
Wordsworth or Emerson, when it comes to putting for
ward the proposition that nature speaks poems and
humble people poetry, it is as true of Whitman as of
Keats or Wordsworth, at their best, that his poetical
contact with raw experience is proved on the pulses. At
this end of the range of his language his words are absolutely true, and this unquestionable authority is exactly
what Whitman wanted to convey. It is as if he is daring
the reader to question the truth of his statement, when
it so clearly bears the touchstone of true experience. It is
as if he were saying: "You would not dare ask the sailor
if he knew how to manage his ship, or the axeman if he
knew how to split the log. Would you dare question my
words?"

On this level, one certainly would not. Consider the
language of a few of a thousand examples, where, in
Whitman's own words, "a perfect user of words uses
things." He watches blacksmiths at work:

> The lithe sheer of their waists plays even with their
>   massive arms,
> Overhand the hammers swing, overhand so slow,
>   overhand so sure. . . .[2]

he watches living things in the country:

> Where the bat flies in the Seventh-month eve, where
>   the great gold-bug drops through the dark,
> Where the brook puts out of the roots of the old tree
>   and flows to the meadow,
> Where cattle stand and shake away flies with the
>   tremulous shuddering of their hides. . . .[2]

he listens to the sounds of the city:

> The blab of the pave, tires of carts, sluff of boot-soles,
>   talk of the promenaders,
> The heavy omnibus, the driver with his interrogating

thumb, the clank of the shod horses on the granite
floor. . . .[4]

ne feels with all his senses:

The hiss of the surgeon's knife, the gnawing teeth of
his saw,
Wheeze, cluck, swash of falling blood, short wild
scream, and long, dull, tapering groan. . . .[5]

ne is peaceful:

Where the splash of swimmers and divers cools the
warm noon,
Where the katy-did works her chromatic reed on the
walnut-tree over the wall,
Through patches of citrons and cucumbers with
silver-wired leaves. . . .[6]

ne takes a straight look at agony:

I am the hounded slave, I wince at the bite of the dogs,
Hell and despair are upon me, crack and again crack
the marksmen,
I clutch the rails of the fence, my gore dribs, thinn'd
with the ooze of my skin.[7]

These are the proofs of the man who was there. The
language oscillates with marvellous sensitivity to the
magnetic object that stirs it, accumulated blunt mono-
syllables, undulating phrases with one adjective sticking
up sharp in the middle, the knock of consonants, the
flow of open vowels.

This is the language of the democratic identity, the one
who shares in clearly delineated experience. The other
identity, of the solitary singer and the visionary poet, has
a language that is both more comprehensive and (in the
sense of the creation of new and startling images) wittier.
A woman's body in childbirth becomes the opening of
doors into life, and death returns again to life:

To his work without flinching the accoucheur comes,
I see the elder-hand pressing receiving supporting,
I recline by the sills of the exquisite flexible doors,
And mark the outlet, and mark the relief and escape.

And as to you Corpse I think you are good manure,
    but that does not offend me,
I smell the white roses sweet-scented and growing,
I reach to the leafy lips, I reach to the polish'd breasts
    of melons.[8]

It is curious to note here affinities with two poems Whitman had probably never read, Andrew Marvell's "Coy Mistress" and "Thoughts in a Garden."

Whitman's passion for observing people is always highly selective and dramatic; he rejects no one, but not for ignorance of what most onlookers would prefer not to see:

This now is too lamentable a face for a man,
Some abject louse asking leave to be, cringing for it,
Some milk-nosed maggot blessing what lets it wrig to
    its hole.

This face is a dog's snout sniffing for garbage,
Snakes nest in that mouth, I hear the sibilant threat.

This face is a haze more chill than the arctic sea,
Its sleepy and wabbling icebergs crunch as they go.[9]

But it is not in isolated short passages that this poetic identity of Whitman's develops its full sweep of imagination and flexible language. It often needs a whole poem for demonstration, "Out of the Cradle endlessly rocking" or the great Lincoln elegy, "When Lilacs last in the Dooryard bloom'd." But "The Sleepers" remains the best poem in which to study the process by which the great poet, not only Whitman, liberates his identity from that of the creature imprisoned in the body, the one who notes, however, beautifully, precise details or sudden drama, who simply exists, however admirable an animal existence may be. What is typical of Whitman's dualism is that the liberated identity, freed of the controls and limits of daily life, finds its highest good in the process of becoming many identities that each enrich some aspect or share of ordinary life.

"The Sleepers"[10] was one of the poems in the original 1855 issue of *Leaves of Grass*; it is a basic source of Whitman's poetic method. The poem opens directly—"I wander all night in my vision"—but this is no medieval dream-allegory, nor is it a symbolic vision like Blake's, though the phrases that follow the opening line are reminiscent of Blake's illustrations to Dante:

> Stepping with light feet, swiftly and noiselessly stepping
>   and stopping,
> Bending with open eyes over the shut eyes of sleepers,
> Wandering and confused, lost to myself, ill-assorted,
>   contradictory,
> Pausing, gazing, bending, and stopping.[11]

"Lost to myself" is the crucial phrase; the poet is in the process of becoming, what he does not yet know, and in the process he will find himself. In a medieval dream-poem or a mystic's vision, what is found is something outside the self, which is revealed in clear and sometimes blinding light. Whitman is at the same time looking at the world of sleeping people and at himself, with the possibility that he can soothe some, for most of the sleepers are wretched, unrequited or condemned, although a little love is allowed.

Now he moves beyond this separate sympathy to a completer identification, he becomes the other dreamers:

> I am a dance—place up there! the fit is whirling me
>   fast![12]

Immediately the poem has become far more complex, and the language follows suit:

Well do they do their jobs those journeymen divine,
Only from me can they hide nothing, and would not if
  they could,
I reckon I am their boss and they make me a pet
  besides,
And surround me and lead me and run ahead when I
  walk,
To lift their cunning covers to signify me with stretch'd
  arms, and resume the way;
Onward we move, a gay gang of blackguards!—with
  mirth-shouting music and wild-flapping pennants
  of joy![13]

The dream has become a ritual of which the sleeping world is the dance, in which nothing is irretrievably good or evil or stuck in the present moment. Sex is freed of its daytime restrictions by the gentle darkness:

I am she who adorn'd herself and folded her hair
  expectantly,
My truant lover has come, and it is dark.

Double yourself and receive me darkness,
Receive me and my lover too, he will not let me go
  without him.

I roll myself upon you as upon a bed, I resign myself to
  the dusk.
He whom I call answers me and takes the place of my
  lover,
He rises with me silently from the bed.

Darkness, you are gentler than my lovers, his flesh was
  sweaty and panting,
I feel the hot moisture yet that he left me.

My hands are spread forth, I pass them in all directions,
I would sound up the shadowy shore to which you are
  journeying.

DEATH AFTER LOVE

Be careful darkness! already what was it touch'd me,
I thought my lover had gone, else darkness and he are
    one,
I hear the heart-beat, I follow, I fade away.[14]

After this moment of love various images of death and
destruction follow, a swimmer is drowned, a ship is
wrecked, the dreamer who is now a spectator of life cannot help. Then follow, as it were, two paintings that the
sleepwalker passes, a stiff little one of George Washington,
and a hopeful but remote one of a Red Indian squaw
who had come to the poet's mother with rushes for making chairs. These were images of light, and in the next
section the poet abruptly states:

I am jealous and overwhelm'd with friendliness,
And will go gallivant with the light and air myself.

O love and summer, you are in the dreams and in
    me. . . .[15]

A different relation is revealed between sleep and
misery, which is that sleep and night average out good
and evil, happy and sad, give a chance of peace and
beauty, and give the soul which is "the myth of heaven"
its chance. The final section is a vision of healing and
renewal, when all the sleepers "pass the invigoration of
the night and the chemistry of the night, and awake."
The dreamer himself addresses night, with all its offerings
of love and death, and promises to return:

I love the rich running day, but I do not desert her
    in whom I lay so long,
I know not how I came of you and I know not where I
    go with you, but I know I came well and shall go
    well.[16]

It is customary nowadays to give this poem the full
psychological treatment, to interpret it as "the descent
of the as yet unformed and unstable ego into the id, its
confrontation there of the dark, human tragedy, its

emergence in a new, more stable form."[17] Many critics have also pointed out that in this, as in many other poems, Whitman has anticipated the stream-of-consciousness theories of the twentieth century. (So, for that matter, had Sterne in the eighteenth.)

It is more useful to regard it in two ways. Firstly it is a poetic experience complete in itself, which the reader must share as he shares "Kubla Khan," as a dream which no explanations can make more complete. Secondly, it is an admirable introduction to Whitman's most successful poetic method. The fluid, merging identity that yet returns unmistakably to the "I" of the poet controls the whole poem; it is imbued with the religious impulse that Whitman always maintained was behind *Leaves of Grass*, however little any revealed religion could claim Whitman; finally it incorporates in its images Whitman's basic and unchanging ideas of the healing nature as well as the torment of sex (a passage in the first edition about adolescent agonies was later removed), and of what might be called positive inertia, the faith that endurance will lead to recovery. All this is faithfully conveyed in language that ranges from American colloquialism to rhapsodic invocation.

The fullest treatment of identity is in Whitman's longest and richest poem, "Song of Myself." In its thirteen hundred and fifty-odd lines (various revisions slightly altered its length) the "I" of the poem lives like a spider in a web of associations. In fact it is worth quoting entire here one of Whitman's most perfect little poems, "A noiseless patient Spider," for the intensely powerful image it conveys of the poet's loneliness and yet his need to connect, as also the freedom and the faith he requires.

A noiseless patient spider,
I mark'd where on a little promontory it stood
    isolated,

Mark'd how to explore the vacant vast surrounding,
It launched forth filament, filament, filament, out of
   itself,
Ever unreeling them, ever tirelessly speeding them.

And you O my soul where you stand,
Surrounded, detached, in measureless oceans of space,
Ceaselessly musing, venturing, throwing, seeking the
   spheres to connect them,
Till the bridge you will need be form'd, till the ductile
   anchor hold,
Till the gossamer thread you fling catch somewhere, O
   my soul.[18]

(This, incidentally, was originally a "Calamus" love-
poem, and entirely reworked, until published in its
present form with "Passage to India.")

"Song of Myself" opens with the celebration of the "I"
of the poem, but this immediately (in the second line)
related to "you"—that is, the ordinary, uncommitted
reader. The sharing with human beings is just as quickly
followed by a sharing with nature:

I loafe and invite my soul,
I lean and loafe at my ease observing a spear of summer
   grass.[19]

It is the typical situation of becoming; existence is going
on, but as yet nothing has been made of it. The second
section is an ecstatic statement of the joy of existence, and
the certainty that, to live properly, "you" will have to
come forward and "filter them from yourself." This,
despite all the complications that ensue, is really the
basic theme of "Song of Myself," the search for the
achievement of a truly living identity. The achievement
of this supremely difficult task is what D. H. Lawrence
honoured so much in Whitman: "the sheer appreciation
of the instant moment, life surging itself at its very
wellhead."[20] Whatever else comes in, whatever knowledge

of death, division or despair, whatever the transcendental vision of further and deeper reality, Whitman is always faithful to the conviction that living is joyful and now. The only complete failure is the failure to "possess the good of the earth and sun." If this is optimism, it is optimism with all the risks calculated, and carried through with the genuine fervour of religion. Whitman refuses to be budged from the present moment:

> I have heard what the talkers were talking, the talk of
>   the beginning and the end,
> But I do not talk of the beginning or the end.[21]

(How very *un*like Mr Eliot!)

But Whitman swiftly goes beyond the elementary simplicities of an "I," a "you," and a "now." The present moment is constantly born, and sex conceived it; in a wonderful phrase he calls sex "a knit of identity."[22] Sex adds a further mystery to every separate being; Whitman elaborates this in one of the best short examples of the capacity of his language to assemble materials with complete confidence and wit:

> Sure as the most certain sure, plumb in the uprights,
>   well entretied, braced in the beams,
> Stout as a horse, affectionate, haughty, electrical,
> I and this mystery here we stand.[23]

The "I" is capable of a whole existence and also of standing apart, observing both its own complications and those of the world, and rushing into sect. 5 Whitman introduces the nearest and furthest mystery, love, which is capable of uniting body and soul and all creation. This section is one of the greatest mystical visions in all poetry; and yet one hesitates to use the word "mystical" about a vision that is also so precise and compassionate, and so perfectly, after the earlier strutting and exaltation, introduces the theme of humility. If a sample is required of Whitman's genius as a poet, to enlighten the

ignorant or to humble the captious, this is the one to
give:

I believe in you my soul, the other I am must not abase
    itself to you,
And you must not be abased to the other.

I mind how once we lay such a transparent summer
    morning,
How you settled your head athwart my hips and
    gently turn'd over upon me,
And parted the shirt from my bosom-bone, and plunged
    your tongue to my bare-stript heart,
And reach'd till you felt my beard, and reach'd till
    you held my feet.

Swiftly arose and spread around me the peace and
    knowledge that pass all the argument of the earth,
And I know that the hand of God is the promise of
    my own,
And I know that the spirit of God is the brother of my
    own,
And that all men ever born are also my brothers, and
    the women my sisters and lovers,

And that a kelson of the creation is love,
And limitless are leaves stiff or drooping in the fields,
And brown ants in the little wells beneath them,
And mossy scabs of the worm fence, heap'd stones,
    elder, mullein and poke-weed.[24]

In these first five sections, the single identity, both "I"
and "you," has been expanded into universal significance, through the joy of living, through sex and through
love. The theme is stated (as it was later in the image of
the spider) that however lonely a man is he cannot live
alone. With this established, Whitman returns to the
image of the "spear of summer grass" that had been
given out in the fifth line of the poem, with the dis-
arming question: "A child said *What is the grass?* fetching

it to me with full hands." Whitman sees it first as the
stuff of life and then, in an extension of the Biblical
metaphor, as "the beautiful uncut hair of graves." The
true identity must also be made up of death.

For the next eight sections Whitman explores images
of life and death. Whitman has been much abused, and
often justly enough, for his catalogues; here the enumera-
tions are entirely appropriate and exquisitely detailed.
The expanded identity of "I" and "you" now shares
life, love, and death, so it must take a long look at what
goes to such a sharing. Everything is included except
guilt and shame; they are simply unnecessary. The
earlier concentration on the purely instinctive and spiritual life is enlarged by a consideration of knowledge and
occupations, with a hint of a further knowledge in nature
itself. The eyes of oxen express "more than all the print I
have read in my life."[25] The original individual identity is
capable of endless response: "I resist anything better
than my own diversity."[26]

At the end of sect. 19, having reached the heart of the
poem, Whitman slyly asks: "Do you guess I have some
intricate purpose?" Those critics who have pictured
Whitman as a vast barbaric open mouth senselessly
pouring forth words must be astonishingly capable of
disregarding his signposts!

Having asked his question, and having stated his
possibilities, he now goes on to settle fair and square on
himself and try and define what he is, not being afraid of
some ironical mockery:

Who goes there? hankering, gross, mystical, nude;
How is it I extract strength from the beef I eat?[27]

Now at last he truly begins to celebrate himself, through
images of the night, the earth, and, above all, the sea.
He tackles the contemporary situation, and welcomes the
modern age, with its science and democracy, and then,
having already routed guilt and shame, sings a hymn of

praise to the sacredness of sex and the unique capacity of
the senses to intensify the living moment. "Copulation is
no more rank to me than death is."[28] Through a series
of sexual images that would be startling at any time, let
alone in the eighteen-fifties, the poem rises to a peak of
ecstasy that rivals that of sect. 5 in intensity and exceeds
it in boldness of imagery:

> That I walk up my stoop, I pause to consider if it
>   really be,
> A morning-glory at my window satisfies me more than
>   the metaphysics of books.
>
> To behold the day-break!
> The little light fades the immense and diaphanous
>   shadows,
> The air tastes good to my palate.
>
> Hefts of the moving world at innocent gambols silently
>   rising, freshly exuding,
> Scooting obliquely high and low.
> Something I cannot see puts upward libidinous prongs,
> Seas of bright juice suffuse heaven.[29]

Any single identity that can be susceptible to such
huge activity must be huge in itself. Whitman gives some
more examples from the senses, this time from hearing,
culminating in a final working of the original notebook
descriptions of Whitman's reaction to the tenor and the
soprano at the opera. But, of all the senses, touch is the
one closest to sex, the one "quivering me to a new
identity";[30] and in sect. 28, despite his earlier refusal to
admit shame or guilt, the poet admits that in giving way
to this auto-erotic passion he is a traitor. The meaning of
this is that in the process of being, in becoming a full and
true identity, the "I" cannot turn in on itself without
narrowing itself; the senses are divine, but they should
radiate outwards, and human beings should be like

animals, they should include and not exclude. Instances of this are given in the following sections.

This brings him to a consideration of the full majesty of identity, which is given vastness by existing in space and time. The catalogue that follows includes everything, nature, industry, human relaxations, the stars, the sun and moon:

> I visit the orchards of spheres and look at the product,
> And look at quintillions ripen'd and look at quintillions green.

> I fly those flights of a fluid and swallowing soul,
> My course runs below the soundings of plummets.[31]

This passage provides yet another example of Whitman's use of language as a force similar in its potency to sex—"a knit of identity"—and equally able to unite the physical and homely with the spiritual.

In his various catalogues of activities Whitman has not yet given space to the qualities needed to cope with them; he is not so naïve as to imagine that the process of becoming is automatic and does not involve the will and the problems of morality. He gives therefore a series of pictures of misfortune or injustice, a shipwreck, martyrs, the burning of witches, the pursuit of escaped slaves, the death of a fireman, war. In the next two sections, there are long and dramatic accounts of a Texas massacre and a sea-fight. These are seen with great sympathy and immediacy, but from the outside. Abruptly in sect. 38 Whitman halts himself:

> Enough! enough! enough!
> Somehow I have been stunn'd. Stand back!
> Give me a little time beyond my cuff'd head, slumbers, dreams, gaping,
> I discover myself on the verge of a usual mistake.

> That I could forget the mockers and insults!
> That I could forget the trickling tears and the blows

of the bludgeons and hammers!
That I could look with a separate look on my own
    crucifixion and bloody crowning!

I remember now,
I resume the overstaid fraction,
The grave of rock multiplies what has been confided
    to it, or to any graves,
Corpses rise, gashes heal, fastenings roll from me.[32]

The self has been repeating the mistake of exclusiveness, although this time in a different way, not by excluding the surrounding world and concentrating on
itself, but by standing apart from the activities of the
world. Only a shadow of an identity can be an un-
involved spectator; Jesus was, above all, involved. Full
existence is only possible through sympathy and love;
some of Whitman's images here are so fundamentally
religious and timeless that they could have been subjects
for Piero della Francesca or Verrocchio:

By the mechanic's wife with her babe at her nipple
    interceding for every person born,
Three scythes at harvest whizzing in a row from three
    lusty angels with shirts bagg'd out at their
    waists, . . .[33]

However, the worst dangers to the good life do not
come from great disasters, but from insidious despairs
and self-satisfied shallowness, from what Blake called
"the idiot questioner." To mock the mockers, Whitman
allows his satirical self to emerge:

Ever myself and my neighbours, refreshing, wicked,
    real,
Ever the old inexplicable query, ever that thorn'd
    thumb, that breath of itches and thirsts,
Ever the vexer's *hoot! hoot!* till we find where the sly
    one hides and bring him forth,
Ever love, ever the sobbing liquid of life,

Ever the bandage under the chin, ever the trestles of
    death. . . .

The little plentiful manikins skipping around in collars
    and tail'd coats,
I am aware who they are, (they are positively not
    worms or fleas,) . . .[34]

The next seven or eight sections recapitulate what has
gone before, being more explicit about religion, which
Whitman sees rather as an inheritance of many religions
than as a directive power, whereas God is present every-
where, and the full identity is God's incarnation:

I hear and behold God in every object, yet understand
    God not in the least,
Nor do I understand who there can be more wonderful
    than myself. . . .[35]

The poem has now curved back to the *dramatis personae*
of the opening, the "I," the "you," the blade of grass,
but they are all connected and the vastness of each has
been revealed. Contradictions do not matter; only the
narrow, excluding man could shut them out. The poem
closes with a final vision, typically composed of the
"now" and the "beyond," expressed in that all-including
language which is also characteristic of Shakespeare at
his most mature, language not nervous of being familiar
and exalted at the same time:

The spotted hawk swoops by and accuses me, he
    complains of my gab and my loitering.

I too am not a bit tamed, I too am untranslatable,
I sound my barbaric yawp over the roofs of the world.

The last scud of day holds back for me,
It flings my likeness after the rest and true as any on
    the shadow'd wilds,
It coaxes me to the vapor and the dusk.

I depart as air, I shake my white locks at the runaway
   sun,
I effuse my flesh in eddies, and drift it in lacy jags.

I bequeath myself to the dirt to grow from the grass I
   love,
If you want me again look for me under your boot-
   soles.

You will hardly know who I am or what I mean,
But I shall be good health to you nevertheless,
And filter and fibre your blood.

Failing to fetch me at first keep encouraged,
Missing me one place search another,
I stop somewhere waiting for you.[36]

It is essential, when discussing Whitman, to deal ex-
tensively with "Song of Myself," not only because it is
one of the most remarkable poems ever written, but
because it reveals the complexity of Whitman's genius
and his quite extraordinary command of language. At one
stage in his last years he said to Traubel: "I sometimes
think the *Leaves* is only a language experiment."[37] In
"Song of Myself" the reader shares not only the excitement of the experiment, but the joy of knowing it to be
successful.

It is primarily a poem of celebration; Whitman says so
himself in the first line. But it also is a work of exploration, an answer, finding itself as it progresses, to the primary questions: "Who and what am I?" The spider
throws out the web of identification until the whole
fabric is formed in time and space. Whitman assembles
here; in other poems he takes apart, or faces up to the
wreckage when a stone from an enemy or a meteor from
heaven crashes through the living web. The affirmation
and the sense of wholeness with which the poem closes
are very dear to Whitman, but he is not ignorant of

F

disintegration, of the difficulty of preserving faith in an
expanding identity. It is easy, from reading Whitman's
bad poems and misreading his good ones, to blame him
for a blind faith in the benefits of forward movement and
omnivorous merging, for a lack of a sense of evil and
corruption, for a disregard of the privacy of a man's soul.
D. H. Lawrence, in the satirical first half of his excellent
essay on Whitman, accused him of being "a pipe open
at both ends, so everything runs through," and ful-
minated against the chant of "One Identity."[38] Yeats,
who had begun as "a boy of seventeen, Walt Whitman
in his pocket," ended by calling Whitman superficial
because he lacked "the Vision of Evil."[39] Whitman anticipated this sort of criticism himself, when he said that
the "introspective, sin-seeking Tolstoy may better represent the present day than I do."[40]

Whitman suffers also in our present day, with its
disproportionate emphasis on tragedy and on the broken,
at the expense of comedy and the whole, at a time when
yea-sayers are regarded with the gravest suspicion. But
Whitman's great affirmation in "Song of Myself" should
be compared rather to the religious virtue of charity; it
is human inadequacy that calls it forth. Whitman is no
mindless ape beating his chest for rude health, nor is he,
like his master Emerson, betrayed into an intellectual
transcendentalism. His language is almost sufficient proof
in itself.

However, as has been stressed in the biographical
study of Whitman, he was brought up in intimate contact with disease, despair, and madness. If he struggles
towards a whole and affirmative identity it is precisely
because he knows what the alternatives are. In the midst
of the sort of pæan of merging which annoyed D. H.
Lawrence, in "Song of the Open Road," Whitman takes
a good look at the implications of what he is saying, in
language that should sound familiar to a Webster, a
Baudelaire, an Eliot:

Behold through you as bad as the rest,
Through the laughter, dancing, dining, supping, of
    people,
Inside of dresses and ornaments, inside of those wash'd
    and trimm'd faces,
Behold a secret silent loathing and despair. . . .

Smartly attired, countenance smiling, form upright,
    death under the breast-bones, hell under the skull-
    bones, . . .[41]

Whitman's ideal of innocent becoming is perfectly
expressed in the beautiful simplicity of the poem "There
was a Child went forth," but even that includes the mean
and unjust father. In a group of several of his finest poems
Whitman deals with the agonising doubts that accompany
the effort to make the broken identity whole. In "As I
ebb'd with the Ocean of Life" (incidentally one of those
lyrics whose tautness of control makes nonsense of the
notion that Whitman had no conception of form), he
surveys himself with absolute honesty, shredding away
all else but the fundamental symbols of the sea-mother
and the land-father, connected by nothing but worthless
sea-drift—

                        . . . those slender windrows,
    Chaff, straw, splinters of wood, weeds, and the sea-
        gluten,
    Scum, scales from shining rocks, leaves of salt-lettuce,
        left by the tide, . . .[42]

He does not shirk the realisation that this, too, is his
identity, and the passage that follows is the test-case for
the assessment of Whitman's optimism as well as for his
egotism:

    O baffl'd, balk'd, bent to the very earth,
    Oppress'd with myself that I have dared to open my
        mouth,

Aware now that amid all that blab whose echoes recoil
      upon me I have not once had the least idea who or
      what I am,
But that before all my arrogant poems the real Me
      stands yet untouched, untold, altogether unreach'd,
Withdrawn far, mocking me with mock-congratulatory
      signs and bows,
With peals of distant ironical laughter at every word I
      have written,
Pointing in silence to these songs, and then to the sand
      beneath.
I perceive I have not really understood any thing, not
      a single object, and that no man ever can,
Nature here in sight of the sea taking advantage of me
      to dart upon me and sting me,
Because I have dared to open my mouth to sing at all.[43]

Fully to appreciate the anguish of this one must take
into consideration the seriousness with which Whitman
took his calling as a poet. He himself drew a parallel
with Milton:

Ever since what might be call'd thought, or the bud-
ding of thought, fairly began in my youthful mind, I
had had a desire to attempt some worthy record of that
entire faith and acceptance ("to justify the ways of
God to man" is Milton's well-known and ambitious
phrase) which is the foundation of moral America.[44]

Already in the same essay he had indicated the austerity
of his task, probably unconsciously echoing Milton's
words:

For grounds for *Leaves of Grass*, as a poem, I abandon'd
the conventional themes, which do not appear in it:
none of the stock ornamentation, or choice plots of
love or war, or high, exceptional personages of Old-
World song; nothing, as I may say, for beauty's sake—
no legend, or myth, or romance, nor euphemism, nor
rhyme.[45]

Whitman, admitting that he, too, is "but a trail of
drift and debris," with all that that implies for the poet,
does not carry on to the next stage of despair, as does
Matthew Arnold in "Dover Beach." In his old age,
Whitman remarked how comforting it was that the Lord
finds a place for all, for the bedbug, the rat, the flea, even
for Matthew Arnold. Something of the same conclusion
saves him here, that

> You up there walking or sitting,
> Whoever you are, we too lie in drifts at your feet.[46]

The ocean must flow as well as ebb, and Whitman, offering love and asking a kiss of the father-land, begging the
sea-mother not to deny him, is left with humility rather
than despair.

Whitman doubts not only himself, but the world on to
which he has projected his identity; he has fears

> Of the terrible doubt of appearances,
> Of the uncertainty after all, that we may be
>   deluded, . . .[47]

Both Whitman's pragmatism and his idealism come to
his assistance when his identity seems to be only a façade,
and evil seems triumphant. His pragmatism enables him
to tackle it as an animal or a farmer does a drought; the
animal hangs on until it dies or gets water, the farmer
sees his appearance of plenty blowing away, but knows
that when the rain comes he will at least have himself.
Similarly, the soldier carries on because there is no point
in brooding over the fact that he may be shot. Whitman's
idealism has given him the Blakean vision of eternity
beyond the failure of materials, which he admits even in
himself.

> It is not upon you alone the dark patches fall,
> The dark threw its patches down upon me also,
> The best I had done seem'd to me blank and suspicious,

My great thoughts as I had supposed them, were they
    not in reality meagre?
Nor is it you alone who know what it is to be evil,
I am he who knew what it was to be evil,
I too knitted the old knot of contrariety,
Blabb'd, blush'd, resented, lied, stole, grudg'd,
Had guile, anger, lust, hot wishes I dared not speak,
Was wayward, vain, greedy, shallow sly, cowardly,
    malignant,
The wolf, the snake, the hog, not wanting in me, . . .[48]

There is a further method of dealing with "the terrible
doubt of appearances," and this is very typical of Whitman, the Whitman who was always pointing out to
people that he was "cautious," "prudent," "furtive."
This was the fact that that identity, in order to cope at
all, must forge itself an outward appearance. Nowadays,
when talk of "the mask" and "the persona" is so fashionable in critical circles that one wonders whether any
writer ever really lived his own experience, one can at
least talk with some safety about Whitman's masks, because he wore them with such effrontery, challenging you
to look beyond them. "One of the roughs," with his
"barbaric yawp," is full of tender secrets:

I give you fair warning before you attempt me further
I am not what you supposed, but far different. . . .[49]

At the end of his life he confessed to Edward Carpenter,
"I think there are truths which it is necessary to envelop
or wrap up";[50] and Carpenter himself noticed in him "a
certain artfulness, combined with keen, penetrating and
determined candour; the wild-hawk look still there,
'untamable, untranslatable,' yet with that wonderful
tenderness at bottom."[51] In this instance, Whitman was
no doubt referring to his homosexual feelings, which he
wished to be kept as a hidden truth: but in all cases he
wished some part of the identity to be kept secret, and for
a mask to be exposed to the wounds and blows of reality,

so that you could no more injure the secret self than you could wound the night or the sea. It is this primitive, secret self that Whitman primarily celebrates, especially in its rituals of love and death, and having dispensed with all myths he manages to state the life of the individual identity so completely that he gives it the universal significance of a myth. Yet the essence of myth is that its hero wears the mask of a secret life; in his heroic battle with the monster he is our secret selves and our secret dreams. Moreover, the tragedies and deaths of myths lead to rebirth, an upsurge of fertility. Whitman's depth and breadth as a poet comes from this instinctive faculty of being able to create a myth of the individual. There are few glimpses of actual love-affairs in Whitman's poems, rather the poems are themselves primitive secret rituals of love and sex; similarly there are few described deaths (those that are, are brilliant) but the poems themselves strip the mask off reality and reveal Blake's invisible worm at the heart of the rose.

For Whitman, death is the profoundest and most cunning wearer of the mask, he knows that

> . . . you beyond them come forth to remain, the rest
>   reality,
> That behind the mask of materials you patiently wait,
>   no matter how long,
> That you will one day perhaps take control of all,
> That you will perhaps dissipate this entire show of
>   appearance,
> That may-be you are what it is all for, but it does not
>   last so very long,
> But you will last very long.[52]

Freud once said to Thornton Wilder, in answer to the suggestion that Shakespeare and Goethe had anticipated his theories: "But the poets have always known them!" This instinctive knowledge of Whitman's is one reason why he makes such fascinating reading in the middle of the twentieth century, when the mysteries of human psychology have been analysed and dissected with a correspondingly agonised growth of that self-consciousness which D. H. Lawrence so bitterly deplored as typical of modern man. Despite all Whitman's exploration of identity, there is a mystery left at the heart of his best work, an area inhabited by unspoken truths. This is one reason why he is such a great poet of death. Others, Donne or George Herbert, for instance, have written great Christian poems of death; others, like Keats or Poe, have written great poems of the morbid terror and fascination of death. But only Whitman has presented death in its mysterious relation to love and rebirth without challenging its mystery or loathing its potency.

Whitman's indifference to salvation or damnation—

> And the threat of what is call'd hell is little or nothing
>   to me,
> And the lure of what is call'd heaven is little or nothing
>   to me. . . .[53]

—has led critics of orthodox belief to imagine that he is indifferent to the problem of death. He is supposed to be like a horse walking past the corpse of a dead horse, presumably aware of the fact of death, but nothing more. But death is at the very heart of Whitman's poetry. The leaves of grass, "the uncut hair of graves," are also his poems that will grow out of his dying body, as lovers die into each other into a beauty that is beyond life:

> O slender leaves! O blossoms of my blood! I permit you
>   you to tell in your own way of the heart that is under,
> O I do not know what you mean there underneath
>   yourselves, you are not happiness,
> You are often more bitter than I can bear, you burn
>   and sting me,
> Yet you are beautiful to me you faint-tinged roots, you
>   make me think of death,

Death is beautiful from you, (what indeed is finally
　beautiful except death and love?)
O I think it is not for life I am chanting here my chant
　of lovers, I think it must be for death,
For how calm, how solemn it grows to ascend to the
　atmosphere of lovers,
Death or life I am then indifferent, my soul declines to
　prefer,
(I am not sure but the high soul of lovers welcomes
　death most,)
Indeed O death, I think now these leaves mean
　precisely the same as you mean,
Grow up taller sweet leaves that I may see! grow up
　out of my breast![54]

Whitman said on several occasions that he was an
"indirect" poet, and despite his brilliant gift for direct
description and statement, this is basically true. His most
complex and moving poems about death are all indirect,
and death in them is incorporated in images of life. The
paradox is typical of Whitman, that the poet of health and
sex should also be the poet of death. No one could have
fought harder against death than Whitman, in his own
life and in his attempts to breathe life into the dying
soldiers of the Washington hospitals. Yet the instinctive
fascination remains, never driven away by the attempt to
force it into a logical form, simply left as a word or an
image. When he attempts to be explicit, as in most of the
poems in *Whispers of Heavenly Death*, Whitman is usually
banal or sententious, he expresses that part of himself
which he has in common with the Californians who
patronise Forest Lawn, or indeed with the ancient Egypt-
ians, in whose customs Whitman was remarkably well-
read. What matters is when Whitman the poet comes into
contact with death.

One could expect that the greatest of these poems
should be involved with the sea, one of the supreme

fertilising symbols of Whitman's life, the intimate associate of his childhood and a source of energy in his old age. "Out of the Cradle endlessly rocking" washes up with the sea-images of birth, death, love, and music. All through Whitman's life as a poet, the elemental rhythm of the sea, its ability to contain both storm and calm, was the great example of what his verse might do. In *Specimen Days* he describes what it means to him.

The attractions, fascinations there are in sea and shore! How one dwells on their simplicity, even vacuity! What is it in us, arous'd by those indirections and directions? That spread of waves and gray-white beach, salt, monotonous, senseless—such an entire absence of art, books, talk, elegance—so indescribably comforting, even this winter day—grim, yet so delicate-looking, so spiritual—striking emotional, impalpable depths, subtler than all the poems, paintings, music, I have ever read, seen, heard. (Yet let me be fair, perhaps it is because I have read those poems and heard that music.)

Even as a boy, I had the fancy, the wish, to write a piece, perhaps a poem, about the sea-shore—that suggesting, dividing line, contact, junction, the solid marrying the liquid—that curious, lurking something, (as doubtless every objective form finally becomes to the subjective spirit,) which means far more than its first mere sight, grand as that is—blending the real and the ideal, and each made portion of the other. Hours, days, in my Long Island youth and early manhood, I haunted the shores of Rockaway or Coney Island, or away east to the Hamptons or Montauk. Once, at the latter place, (by the old light-house, nothing but sea-tossings in sight in every direction as far as the eye could reach,) I remember well, I felt that I must one day write a book expressing this liquid, mystic theme. Afterward, I recollect, how it came to me that instead of any special lyrical or epical or literary attempt, the sea-shore should be an invisible *influence*, a pervading gauge and tally for me, in my composition.[55]

Whitman is no sailor, no Melville nor Conrad; he walks up and down the sea-shore where life begins, "the solid marrying the liquid." (As always, the sexual symbol comes first with Whitman, so very different from Melville and Conrad.) But symbols of death are also close by, almost there in the fascination with "simplicity, even vacuity . . . monotonous, senseless." And "Out of the Cradle endlessly rocking" is a highly complex dramatic lyric which fulfils Whitman's youthful dream of "expressing this liquid, mystic theme." Indeed, the words "liquid, mystic," describe the structure and content of the poem.

It has often been observed that the poem has a musical structure, containing recitative, aria, and chorus; in fact Whitman first pointed this out himself, in his original anonymous puff for the poem when it was published (in its original version) in the *Saturday Press*, and in his defence of it when it was attacked in a Cincinnati paper. He wrote that "the purport of this wild and plaintive song, well-enveloped, and eluding definition, is positive and unquestionable, like the effect of music."[56] Any discussion of it must take into account this suggestibility which it does share with music, and which makes it essential to treat it as an organic structure.

The tremendous opening sentence, twenty-two lines long, brings the man back to the little boy who wandered out under the yellow half-moon on the Long Island shore. This image of joyful loneliness is given for companion the image of joyful birth and love in the two mocking-birds from Alabama who have come north to make their nest on the shore and hatch forth four light-green eggs spotted with brown. Their wonderful aria is the simplicity of joy:

Shine! shine! shine!
Pour down your warmth, great sun!
While we bask, we two together.

Two together!
Winds blow south, or winds blow north,
Day come white, or night come black,
Home, or rivers and mountains from home,
Singing all time, minding no time,
While we two keep together.[57]

Destruction is indicated with equal simplicity. The she-bird disappears, maybe killed, and the he-bird is left alone:

He call'd on his mate,
He pour'd forth the meanings which I of all men know.[58]

Earlier in the poem, the child carefully watching and not disturbing the birds at the nest was said to be "translating." Now the poet as a man translates the notes of the bird, his brother—

Recalling now the obscure shapes, the echoes, the
    sounds and sights after their sorts,
The white arms out in the breakers tirelessly tossing,
I, with bare feet, a child, the wind wafting my hair,
Listen'd long and long.[59]

The aria that follows, pure and ecstatic, is of "love in the heart long pent, now loose, now at last tumultuously bursting," the awakening of the boy's soul by the song of the bird and the noises of sea and land. But the boy is also a poet, "the outsetting bard." With superlative artistry Whitman has described not only the awakening of love but the awakening of the need to sing, and the bird is both demon and bird. The boy is changed for ever:

Never more shall I escape, never more the
    reverberations,

Never more the cries of unsatisfied love be absent from
   me,
Never again leave me to be the peaceful child I was
   before what there in the night,
By the sea under the yellow and sagging moon,
The messenger there arous'd, the fire, the sweet hell
   within,
The unknown want, the destiny of me.[60]

As with "Song of Myself," this is a poem of becoming,
the boy into the man, the mute watcher into the poet, in
fact the very process of poetry is revealed. Initiated into
life, the awakened poet wants some further answer:

O give me the clew! (it lurks in the night here
   somewhere,)
O if I am to have so much, let me have more!)[61]

The magnificent ending of the poem, giving from the
sea "the word death" as the answer, never openly refers
back to the beginning, when the bird lost its mate and
sang, bringing love and death together, but its introduction of death is inevitable. The opening sentence of the
poem moved into the mysteries of life, the two closing
sentences move into the mystery of death. The beauty of
movement is essential to all Whitman's best poetry,
he shares this quality with life itself, that nothing can
possibly remain static with him; with instinctive sym-
metry Whitman returns to the image of the cradle,
death-in-life, life-in-death, rocked by the old crone, the
fierce old mother, the sea:

Whereto answering, the sea,
Delaying not, hurrying not,
Whisper'd me through the night, and very plainly
   before daybreak,
Lisp'd to me the low and delicious word death,
And again death, death, death, death,
Hissing melodious, neither like the bird nor like my
   arous'd child's heart,

But edging near as privately for me rustling at my feet,
Creeping thence steadily up to my ears and laving me
    softly all over,
Death, death, death, death, death.

Which I do not forget,
But fuse the song of my dusky demon and brother,
That he sang to me in the moonlight on Paumanok's
    gray beach,
With the thousand responsive songs at random,
My own songs awaked from that hour,
And with them the key, the word up from the waves,
The word of the sweetest song and all songs,
That strong and delicious word which, creeping to my
    feet,
(Or like some old crone rocking the cradle, swathed in
    sweet garments, bending aside,)
The sea whisper'd me.[62]

"Out of the Cradle endlessly rocking" is Whitman's most
perfect poem. The elegiac theme that is blended here into
the lyric form emerges to dominate the great poem for
the death of President Lincoln, "When Lilacs last in the
Dooryard bloom'd." Despite its majestic movement, this
poem has not quite the same inevitability as the earlier
work; nevertheless it has the same musical subtlety, the
three themes running together, the solitary aria, the
orchestrated background, and the same quality of
"eluding definition." Above all, it is a most wonderful
poem of death.

It is not like any other elegy, and in one sense it is not
an elegy at all, but a hymn to "sane and sacred death."
Once again, one feels that all Whitman's awful mistakes
were justified; they were the slag from which emerges
the extraordinary originality of poems like "When Lilacs
last. . . ." Whitman's conception of identity admits the
senses into his poems with a freedom they enjoy in the
work, say, of Keats: but in Whitman's insistence on the

equal rights of body and soul the sensual elements never
dominate or become cloying. Here the senses match the
soul in their influence on the poem; they are the introduction to the three symbols, lilac, star, and bird, which
in turn introduce death in terms of the natural cycle, of
individual mourning, and of mystic rapture. The lack
of inevitability is noticeable only at the very beginning,
when after the classic proportion of the opening lines—

> When lilacs last in the dooryard bloom'd,
> And the great star early droop'd in the western sky in
>   the night,
> I mourn'd, and yet shall mourn with ever-returning
>   spring. . . .[63]

—the poet naturally develops further references to star
and lilac, only to jump rather suddenly in sect. 4 to the
hermit-thrush singing in the swamp. Nevertheless, the
shock of this introduction is justified later. After the
dramatically-delayed appearance of the coffin on its
journey "over the breast of spring," through the States
standing like mourning women, through the profusion of
nature as represented by the lilac, suddenly, in sect. 7,
Whitman broadens the whole scope of what had seemed
an elegy for one man (classically not mentioned by name)
by announcing his intention to bring his blossoms and
branches to all the dead, even further, to "chant a song
for you O sane and sacred death." The hermit-thrush then
reappears, and begins to emerge as the symbol of this
further chant, before which the poet delays a moment
longer while "The star my departing comrade holds and
detains me." For this moment the poet sings of the placid
beauty of America, prosperous and fertile under the
"most excellent sun," in a description that is deliberately
generalised in terms that would have pleased even Dr
Johnson; the streak of a tulip here would have spoiled
everything. Then, at last, Whitman can return to the
bird and move beyond temporary sadness for an indi-

vidual to death as peace, an ocean of bliss. The poem
rises from solemnity to exaltation:

> Then with the knowledge of death as walking one side
>   of me,
> And the thought of death close-walking the other side
>   of me,
> And I in the middle as with companions, and as holding
>   the hands of companions.
> I fled forth to the hiding receiving night that talks not,
> Down to the shores of the water, the path by the swamp
>   in the dimness,
> To the solemn shadowy cedars and ghostly pines so
>   still.
> And the singer so shy to the rest receiv'd me,
> The gray-brown bird I know receiv'd us comrades
>   three,
> And he sang the carol of death and a verse for him I
>   love.
>
> From deep secluded recesses,
> From the fragrant cedars and the ghostly pines so still,
> Came the carol of the bird.
>
> And the charm of the carol rapt me,
> As I held as if by their hands my comrades in the night,
> And the voice of my spirit tallied the song of the bird.[11]

The aria that follows, with its vision of death as a soothing
mother, is the means of conferring peace on further
troubled visions. The interwoven senses of the poem—
sight-star, scent-lilac, hearing-bird—are transcended as
the song of the bird enables the poet to see clearly that
after all the carnage of the war, "the white skeletons of
young men," has left anguish to the living; the dead do
not suffer. He passes beyond the victorious bird, the
hopeful lilac "with heart-shaped leaves . . . returning
with spring," "the lustrous and drooping star," and yet
keeps them as he keeps his dead comrade, "their memory

ever to keep." At the end the three symbols of death are
united with the poet—

> and this for his dear sake,
> Lilac and star and bird twined with the chant of my
>   soul,
> There in the fragrant pines and the cedars dusk and
>   dim.[65]

It is useless to compare this poem with other elegies,
to wish it were more clearly tragic, or that it had developed the theme of immortality; even one of Whitman's
most sympathetic critics, Richard Chase, speaks of its
"artificiality," an extraordinary word to use of a poem so
cunningly built of living symbols. Nor is it just to com-
plain that the only person to emerge in the poem is the
poet himself. The poem is typical of Whitman's best
in the swift fertility of its growth, its movement out
and forward; and, as usual, the "I" of the poem gives a
sense of immediacy by living intensely through the growth
of the poem. Whitman is not so much concerned with
tragedy as with the life that follows on death, not with
personal immortality but with the proof death offers that
there is beyond real existence an ideal that is a final
moment of love,

> And the soul turning to thee O vast and well-veil'd death,
> And the body gratefully nestling to thee.[66]

The symbols of the poem are satisfying on every level;
if the argument of the poem remains well-veiled, so does
its subject.

"Out of the Cradle . . ." and "When Lilacs last . . ."
are Whitman's two great hymns to death, and in each
case the final song of praise is reached through the
awakening of love. Some of the best and simplest of
Whitman's poems are concerned with the interplay
between love and death, when he keeps "Vigil of silence,
love and death, vigil for you my son and my soldier."

G

There are enough bad poems in *Drum-Taps* to justify most of Henry James's youthful strictures, but the best ones convey all the agony of the charity (in the Biblical sense) which Whitman displayed in those years as hospital visitor and wound-dresser. He sees both the truth and the sadness of the fact that war calls forth a comradely love that would prevent wars if only prolonged into peace. Whitman both suffers and forgives; there are many examples, utterly simple and moving (such as "As toilsome I wander'd Virginia's Woods") or dramatic and emotional (such as "A Sight in Camp"). But the most succinct and timeless is "Reconciliation":

> Word over all, beautiful as the sky,
> Beautiful that war and all its deeds of carnage must in
>   time be utterly lost,
> That the hands of the sisters Death and Night
>   incessantly softly wash again, and ever again, this
>   soil'd world;
> For my enemy is dead, a man divine as myself is dead,
> I look where he lies white-faced and still in the coffin—I
>   draw near,
> Bend down and touch lightly with my lips the white
>   face in the coffin.[67]

Whitman moved more easily from love to death than he did from love to sex. When he announces himself as "chanter of Adamic songs . . . Bathing myself, bathing my songs in Sex," he raises the uncomfortable suspicion that he is a crank and that sex is nothing more than a programme. Lawrence, with justice, made fun of a lover so generalised that he can say: "I am he that aches with amorous love."[68] Nevertheless, Whitman's praise of sex is profoundly important, not only for itself but considered in its context of nineteenth-century literature. Henry Adams was right in seeing that Whitman alone among American writers had expressed the dynamic force of sex "as every classic had always done."[69] We are only just catching up with the spiritual significance of Whitman's celebration of sex, as D. H. Lawrence found out sixty years after *Leaves of Grass*. Much of Whitman's range and vigour comes from his grasp of the primal significance of sex. The extraordinary image of dawn with its "libidinous prongs" has already been quoted. An equally powerful one is in "I sing the Body Electric":

> Bridegroom night of love working surely and softly
>   into the prostrate dawn,
> Undulating into the willing and yielding day,
> Lost in the cleave of the clasping and sweet-flesh'd day.[70]

These metaphors indicate that Whitman's praise of sex is not just a matter of asserting that the body is sacred, however important that is. For him sex operates on the deepest instinctive levels, deep as the sea and the night, and his unusual capacity to draw from these levels makes him a great poet of sex precisely when he is being least oratorical and deliberate about it. Yet together with his images of sex there is an ability to draw sex into the instant moment, to quiver the "I" and the "you" into a new identity.

For sheer immediacy, the "I" predominates, as might be expected in one of Whitman's sexual character. The "Children of Adam" poems that caused all the fuss in Whitman's lifetime could only be called obscene by those who, in D. H. Lawrence's phrase, like to "tickle the dirty little secret." The poems that were most objected to by Whitman's contemporaries, such as "A Woman waits for Me," are gauchely solemn and painfully passionate: "I pour the stuff to start sons and daughters fit for these States, I press with slow rude muscle." One can hardly be moved to anything but laughter by this aspect of Whitman's sexuality. Nor does he make much poetry out of his praise of nakedness; one feels that it pleases Whitman more as an image of equality and democracy than of sex:

> The man's body is sacred and the woman's body is
> sacred,
> No matter who it is, it is sacred—is it the meanest one
> in the laborer's gang?
> Is it one of the dull-faced immigrants just landed on
> the wharf?
> Each belongs here or anywhere just as much as the
> well-off, just as much as you,
> Each has his or her place in the procession.[71]

Admirable sentiments, well expressed, but entirely lacking in the primal surge of image and language that is the
mark of Whitman's best poetry.

Nor does he succeed any better when he writes about
an allegedly loved person; he usually writes much worse:

> O for you whoever you are your correlative body![72]

But when the indirect old sly poet turns to himself, out
come the real poems—

> The poems of the privacy of the night, and of men like
> me
> This poem drooping shy and unseen that I always
> carry, and that all men carry[73]

—and then the bold miracles begin to flower from the
poetic identity. What other poet would dare to compare
a poem to his penis!

This is the celebratory Whitman, caught as always in
his auto-erotic moments between ecstasy and shame,
uniting opposites of language and imagery, writing
poetry:

> The curious roamer the hand roaming all over the
> body, the bashful withdrawing of flesh where the
> fingers soothingly pause and edge themselves,
> The limpid liquid within the young man,
> The vex'd corrosion so pensive and so painful,

The torment, the irritable tide that will not be at rest,
The like of the same I feel, the like of the same in
    others,
The young man that flushes and flushes, and the
    young woman that flushes and flushes,
The young man that wakes deep at night, the hot hand
    seeking to repress what would master him,
The mystic amorous night, the strange half-welcome
    pangs, visions, sweats,
The pulse pounding through palms and trembling
    encircling fingers, the young man all color'd, red,
    asham'd, angry;
The souse upon me of my lover the sea, as I lie willing
    and naked,
The merriment of the twin babies that crawl over the
    grass in the sun, the mother never turning her
    vigilant eyes from them,
The walnut-trunk, the walnut-husks, and the ripening
    or ripen'd long-round walnuts,
The continence of vegetables, birds, animals,
The consequent meanness of me should I skulk or find
    myself indecent, while birds and animals never once
    skulk or find themselves indecent. . . .[74]

"Visions, sweats"—this is the authentic Whitman mix-ture, they are the soul and body through which sex knits its identity.

There are no images of the beloved in "Children of Adam," although there are poems of lovers moving away from society, escaping together. There is also a strange reference to Whitman's odd habits of roaming the low haunts of the Bowery with his rough friends:

To-day I go consort with Nature's darlings, to-night
    too,
I am for those who believe in loose delights, I share the
    midnight orgies of young men,
I dance with the dancers and drink with the drinkers,

> The echoes ring with our indecent calls, I pick out
>   some low person for my dearest friend,
> He shall be lawless, rude, illiterate, he shall be one
>   condemned by others for deeds done,
> I will play a part no longer, why should I exile myself
>   from my companions?[75]

The reference to playing a part is significant; his conviction of the rightness of the part is not to be questioned, sex *is* sacred: but, to be lost in the elemental dance, as he was in "The Sleepers," he needs either solitude or the companionship of men, and finally a liberating vision of universal love, as in the great passage from "Song of Myself" already quoted ("I mind how once we lay such a transparent summer morning.") Whitman is a revolutionary writer in his treatment of sex, and his integrity remained unshaken in his loyalty to everything he had written about sex. He considered that the true function of the poet was to mediate between nature and man, and therefore the poet should be as honest about sex as nature is. Three years before his death Whitman made a remark to Traubel which is as interesting in its first half as in its second: "Had I Leaves of Grass to write over again, knowing what I know now, I do not think I should in any way touch or abate the sexual portions, as you call them: but in the other matter, in the good and evil business, I should be more definite, more emphatic, than ever."[76] It was at about the same time that he was so shocked by Symonds' demand that he be more definite and emphatic (Whitman's words do very well) about the meaning of the "Calamus" poems!

These poems convince with their passion as most of those in "Children of Adam" do not, telling

> the secret of my nights and days,
> To celebrate the needs of comrades.[77]

The heterosexual poems in "Children of Adam" *cannot*

pass from sex to love; the homosexual poems of "Calamus" are not *allowed* to pass from love to sex. They are indirect, they do not put "my felt and not said things into words." He admits their indirection, and also the fact that they are the most revealing of all his poems:

> Here the frailest leaves of me and yet my strongest
>   lasting,
> Here I shade and hide my thoughts, I myself do not
>   expose them,
> And yet they expose me more than all my other poems.[78]

The furthest sensuality allowed in these poems is a comradely kiss or a holding of hands; not even the Boston puritans found anything to object to in "Calamus." After all, poems written by homosexual poets to their friends had been sanctioned since the time of the Greeks. But the Whitman who occasionally confessed his tortures in his notebooks also hinted in his poems at the effort involved in sublimating homosexual passion into the love of comrades. Whitman compares himself to the earth, "so impassive, ample," yet nourishing its secret volcanoes; so it is with the poet, the lover who touches his friend with a chaste hand, calmly:

> But toward him there is something fierce and terrible
>   in me eligible to burst forth,
> I dare not tell it in words, not even in these songs.[79]

The phallic calamus-plant, growing in the swamps, points up to the sky, connecting the real and the ideal. Whitman was aware of the unsavoury mess of the swamp, but it was in his nature to move up and away, and none of his misgivings could fault his faith in the ideal, the "fervid comradeship" that will be the "counterbalance and offset of our materialistic and vulgar American democracy, and . . . the spiritualization thereof."[80]

Whatever the erotic basis of his attitudes, Whitman is genuinely the poet of the common man. There is no suspicion of a taint of a political programme in him, as socialists and communists have found to their cost when they have tried to appropriate him. With the gregariousness and love of spectacle of a city-dweller, he was as much a child of nature as his favourites in poetry or fiction, Burns or Natty Bumppo; he thought "Natty peculiarly a Leaves of Grass man." But, at the same time, Whitman was neither a proletarian, nor was he content with simple nature. Of Burns he said, after praising his wonderful qualities: "He has . . . little or no spirituality. This last is his mortal flaw and defect, tried by highest standard." Whitman's joy in things as they are, and in men as they are, is always saved from the flatness of materialism by the huge demands of his search for identity, a search ranging from the darkness of instinct to the radiance of the spirit. Whitman's notions of change, of movement, and of becoming, do not degenerate into a naïve belief in progress (despite lapses); he always remains also the one who "loafes," who accepts the fallen and unfallen, nature as it is, who says:

> [I] do not call the tortoise unworthy because she is not
>   something else,
> And the jay in the woods never studied the gamut, yet
>   trills pretty well to me,
> And the look of the bay mare shames silliness out of
>   me.[81]

With all his deliberate exploitation of his personality, he bears no relation to a Rousseau or a Boswell. The reader who is put off by the picture of Walt on stilts, like a barker at a fair, blowing his trumpet and shouting "Look at ME!" should read on, and then he will find that Whitman has astonishing reserves of the true humility that finds its outlet in sympathy and understanding. But, after all, he does write about the great poet, and thus about himself, better than anyone else could:

Now he has passed that way, see after him! There is not left any vestige of despair, or misanthropy, or cunning, or exclusiveness, or the ignominy of a nativity or color, or delusion of hell or the necessity of hell. ... The greatest poet does not moralize or make applications of morals—he knows the soul. The soul has that measureless pride which consists in never acknowledging any lessons or deductions but its own. But it has sympathy as measureless as its pride, and the one balances the other, and neither can stretch too far while it stretches in company with the other. The inmost secrets of art sleep with the twain. The greatest poet has lain close betwixt both, and they are vital in his style and thoughts.[82]

REFERENCES

1. "Song of Myself," § 1. *C.W.*, I. 33.

2. "Song of Myself," § 12. *C.W.*, I. 46.

3. "Song of Myself," § 33. *C.W.*, I. 74.

4. "Song of Myself," § 8. *C.W.*, I. 42.

5. "Song of Myself," § 36. *C.W.*, I. 86.

6. "Song of Myself," § 33. *C.W.*, I. 76-7.

7. "Song of Myself," § 33. *C.W.*, I. 80.

8. "Song of Myself," § 49. *C.W.*, I. 106.

9. "Faces." *C.W.*, II. 245.

10. *C.W.*, II. 201-12.

11. *C.W.*, II. 201.

12. *C.W.*, II. 202.

13. *C.W.*, II. 203.

14. *C.W.*, II. 203-4.

15. *C.W.*, II. 208.

16. *C.W.*, II. 211.

17. Richard Chase, *Walt Whitman Reconsidered*, London 1955, p. 54.

18. *C.W.*, II. 229-30.

19. *C.W.*, I. 33.

20. Introduction to *New Poems*, New York 1920. Reprinted in *Selected Literary Criticism*, ed. A. Beal, London 1955, p. 87.

21. *C.W.*, I. 35.

22. *Ibid.*

23. *C.W.*, I. 36.

24. *C.W.*, I. 38.

25. *C.W.*, I. 47.

26. *C.W.*, I. 54.

27. *C.W.*, I. 56.

28. *C.W.*, I. 63.

29. *C.W.*, I. 64-5.

30. *C.W.*, I. 68.

31. *C.W.*, I. 78.
32. *C.W.*, I. 87–8.
33. *C.W.*, I. 91–2.
34. *C.W.*, I. 93, 94.
35. *C.W.*, I. 105.
36. *C.W.*, I. 108–9.
37. Quoted in F. O. Matthiessen, *American Renaissance*, N.Y. and London 1941, p. 517.
38. D. H. Lawrence, *Selected Literary Criticism*, ed. A. Beal, p. 395.
39. W. B. Yeats, *Autobiographies*, London 1955, p. 246.
40. Quoted in Matthiessen, *American Renaissance*, p. 591.
41. *C.W.*, I. 188.
42. *C.W.*, I. 14.
43. *C.W.*, I. 15.
44. "A Backward Glance o'er Travell'd Roads." *C.W.*, III. 63.
45. *C.W.*, III. 45.
46. "As I Ebb'd with the Ocean of Life." *C.W.*, II. 17.
47. "Of the terrible Doubt of Appearances." *C.W.*, II. 17.
48. "Crossing Brooklyn Ferry." *C.W.*, I. 195.
49. *C.W.*, I. 140.
50. Carpenter, *Days with Walt Whitman*, p. 43.
51. *Op. cit.*, p. 51.
52. "Scented Herbage of my Breast." *C.W.*, I. 139.
53. "As I Lay with my Head in your Lap Camerado." *C.W.*, II. 88.
54. "Scented Herbage of my Breast." *C.W.*, I. 138.
55. *C.W.*, IV. 166–7.
56. Quoted in *S.S.*, p. 231.
57. *C.W.*, II. 7.
58. *C.W.*, II. 8.
59. *C.W.*, II. 8–9.
60. *C.W.*, II. 12.
61. *C.W.*, II. 13.
62. Ibid.
63. *C.W.*, II. 94.
64. *C.W.*, II. 100–1.
65. *C.W.*, II. 104.
66. *C.W.*, II. 102.
67. *C.W.*, II. 87.
68. *C.W.*, II. 133.
69. Quoted in Matthiessen, *American Renaissance*, p. 524.
70. *C.W.*, I. 118.
71. *C.W.*, I. 119.
72. *C.W.*, I. 111.
73. *C.W.*, I. 127.
74. "Spontaneous Me." *C.W.*, I. 128–9.
75. "Nature Moments." *C.W.*, I. 133–4.
76. *W.W.C.*, IV. 389.
77. *C.W.*, I. 137.
78. *C.W.*, I. 156.
79. "Earth, my Likeness." *C.W.*, I. 158.
80. "Democratic Vistas." *C.W.*, V. 131.
81. "Song of Myself," §13. *C.W.*, I. 47.
82. Preface to 1855 edn. of *Leaves of Grass. C.W.*, V. 164, 169–70.

CHAPTER III

THE CRITICS

Whitman has suffered grievously both from his disciples and from his hostile critics; it is a curious irony that his worst poems have been the texts for both groups. The Prophet of Democracy, the Seer of Cosmic Consciousness, the Bard of America was created from the wearisome catalogues of "Salut au Monde" or "A Song of Occupations," from the vague enthusiasms of "Passage to India," "A Song of Joys," or "A Song of the rolling Earth," the Yankee arrogance of "Song of the Exposition." Although there is poetry scattered about in all of these, there is also more than enough bad verse to make the most ardent lover of Whitman flinch. Whitman's failures nearly always occur when he is trying to be an orator instead of a poet. Sometimes it seems that Whitman should have worn the mask of the Old Southern Gambler, ceaselessly shuffling his cards of identity; whenever he wants to put something over on you, he deals the card of the orator. When he is performing as an orator, not only does his language and imagery become crude and flat, but his vital subtlety of rhythm fails him.

Whitman's versification has also been a favourite target of hostile criticism. Perhaps the severest handicap he has had to suffer in the twentieth century has been T. S. Eliot's magisterial but off-hand pronouncement in 1928:

Whitman's originality is both genuine and spurious. It is genuine in so far as it is a *logical* development of certain English prose; Whitman was a great prose writer. It is spurious in so far as Whitman wrote in a way that asserted that his great prose was a new form of verse.[1]

In the exclusive warfare of modern criticism he has been forcibly enlisted amongst the enemy, set up against volleys of fire directed from the fortresses of Baudelaire, Hawthorne, Melville, Henry James, T. S. Eliot. Yet not only are such conflicts even more pointless than most wars, they are riddled with spies and deserters. Henry James had a profound admiration for "dear old Walt"; T. S. Eliot's debt to Whitman has been exposed at length in a book to be referred to later. In short, as Leslie A. Fiedler has said in a brilliant recent essay on Whitman, "he is a poet whom we must begin now to rescue from parody as well as apotheosis."[2]

The irony of Whitman's early reception in America has already been outlined. Apart from the great exception of Emerson, and a slowly growing band of admirers, the poet of American democracy was rejected by Americans. Whitman's career is fascinatingly relevant to more recent democracies, such as Australia; a national myth of independence, generosity, and freedom from humbug, is constantly being made to look absurd by outbreaks of narrow, servile, humourless conformism. Whitman in America was an early victim of that fear of freedom that has subsequently been analysed by writers like Erich Fromm and David Riesmann. Writing to Rudolf Schmidt in Copenhagen in 1872, Whitman indulged in some straight talking that is only slightly exaggerating the truth:

When you are composing your review, I would like to have you bring in, in the proper place, the following mentioned facts—that neither my book of poems or *Democratic Vistas* is cordially accepted in the United States—nor do any of the chief Literary persons or organs of that country admit *Leaves of Grass* as having (possessing) any value or recognize the author as a

poet at all— . . . that, up to this time, no American
publisher will publish it (the author having had to
print its various editions himself)—that many of the
bookstores refuse to keep it for sale—and that the posi-
tion of the author both as to literary rank and worldly
prosperity, in his own country, has been and remains
to day under a heavy and depressing cloud.

Whitman's buoyant nature reasserted itself at the end of
this letter, when he added the note:

Upon reading over my letter, previous to mailing it, I
had almost decided not to send it as a part of it may be
open to the suspicion of querulousness—yet as nothing
can be further from my real state of mind (which is
more than satisfied with my literary fortune upon the
whole) I will let it go.[3]

Nevertheless the rejection was clear enough, ranging
from "chief Literary persons" such as Whittier or Lowell
to the poet's own family:

My brother George once said to me: "Walt, hasn't the
world made it plain that it'd rather not have your
book? Why, then, don't you call the game off?" I
couldn't give George any reason he would have understood. . . . I said nothing.[4]

The best that Whitman could hope for from cultured
Americans was the sort of review that Charles Eliot
Norton wrote of the first edition of *Leaves of Grass*, in
Putnam's Magazine.[5] He praised Whitman for his perception of nature, his manliness, and his directness, but refused to allow either his language or his poetic treatment
of his own identity.

Whitman's critical welcome in England from William
Rossetti, Swinburne, and Mrs Gilchrist meant an enormous amount to the poet, but he was also attacked as
fiercely and praised as lukewarmly as he had been in

America. The main objections in 1856 were that Whitman was both obscene and democratic to excess. *The Saturday Review* advised its readers to "throw them [the poems] instantly behind the fire."[6] The *Critic* produced the authentic tones of outraged gentility:

Walt Whitman is as unacquainted with art, as a hog is with mathematics.... We, who are not prudish, emphatically declare that the man who wrote page 79 of *Leaves of Grass* deserves nothing so richly as the public executioner's whip.[7]

G. H. Lewes allocated praise and blame rather as Charles Eliot Norton had done, although the Englishman allowed himself to be a little warmer:

Walt is one of the most amazing, one of the most startling, one of the most perplexing, creations of the modern American mind; but he is no fool, though abundantly eccentric, nor is his book mere food for laughter, though undoubtedly containing much that may most easily and fairly be turned into ridicule.... Especially do we deplore the unnecessary openness with which Walt reveals to us matters which ought rather to remain in a sacred silence. It is good not to be ashamed of Nature; it is good to have an all-inclusive charity; but it is good, sometimes, to leave the veil across the Temple.[8]

Rossetti's expurgated edition of 1868 still aroused complaints of "glaring and rampant obscenity," but the essence of educated Victorianism appears in Alfred Austin's review in *Temple Bar*:

As Mr Rossetti reminds us, it has been said of Mr Whitman by one of his warmest admirers, "He is Democracy." We really think he is—in his compositions, at least; being, like it, ignorant, sanguine, noisy, coarse, and chaotic! Democracy may be, and we fear is, our proximate future; and it will, as a matter of course, bring its poetry along with it. The prospect is not an agreeable one; but, as a protection both against it and our present condition (of poetry), we can always fall back upon the grand old masters of the Past, from whom it is quite certain that singers, whether insipid or insane, will never succeed in weaning the healthy opinion of mankind.[9]

There are two curious facts about these reviews. One is that they contain the seeds of most future attacks on Whitman and on the form and manner of poetry that he stands for; T. S. Eliot has a lot in common with Alfred Austin. The second is that those writers who are most concerned with the health of the whole man are nearly always accused of sickness and obscenity. It is easy to see why the Victorians were shocked by Whitman's sexual themes and language, as easy as it is to see that we are not shocked by them at all; it is not so easy to explain away the treatment of D. H. Lawrence in our own time. The release of *Lady Chatterley's Lover* in America, England, and Scotland (if not in countries like Eire and Australia) does not seem so very liberal when one considers that not even the Boston censor succeeded in actually *banning* Whitman's *Leaves of Grass*.

The English reviewers voiced their doubts or hostility in the editorial "we." The really important reactions came in the voices of individuals. Swinburne in 1862 wrote to Monckton Milnes: "*Leaves of Grass* . . . is really the most lovely and wonderful thing I have read for years and years."[10] At the end of his essay on Blake, Swinburne spoke out in public with equal enthusiasm, and he also addressed Whitman directly (or Whitman as the apostle of freedom and man) in verse:

> Send but a song overseas for us,
>   Heart of their hearts who are free,
> Heart of their singer, to be for us

> More than our singing can be;
> Ours, in the tempest at error
> With no light but the twilight of terror;
> Send us a song oversea![11]

Even Swinburne was bound to bump down a little from those heights, and his "attack" on Whitman in 1872 was not an attack on the poet, for whom again he declared his "ardent and sympathetic admiration," but on what he called "the formalist," who speaks

> not as though he must but as though he ought; as though it behoved one who would be the poet of American democracy to do this thing or be that thing if the duties of that office were to be properly fulfilled, the tenets of that religion worthily delivered. Never before was high poetry so puddled and adulterated with mere doctrine in its crudest form.[12]

Few balanced critics of Whitman could quarrel with this judgment.

For many of the English writers of this period, coming as they were to a new aestheticism at the tired end of Romanticism, Whitman was a liberator and a healer. The clearest account of this rejuvenating power is given by John Addington Symonds. Symonds describes himself as a sickly young man, educated as an English gentleman at Harrow and Oxford, "decidedly academical, and in danger of becoming a prig." Then Frederic Myers read him aloud a poem from *Leaves of Grass*, he immediately procured a copy of the book, and he experienced a kind of religious conversion. Whitman's poems enabled him to face the problems of sex and the uncouthness of democracy as he never had before:

> He gave body, concrete vitality, to the religious creed which I had been already forming for myself upon the study of Goethe, Greek and Roman Stoics, Giordano Bruno, and the founders of the evolutionary doctrine. He inspired me with faith, and made me feel that

optimism was not unreasonable. This gave me great
cheer in those evil years of enforced idleness and intellectual torpor which my health imposed upon me.
Moreover, he helped to free me from many conceits and
pettinesses to which academical culture is liable. . . .[13]

It is a remarkable tribute (there is a lot more of it,
unquoted), and could scarcely be more remote from
university criticism of the mid-twentieth century. Yet,
as Symonds is at pains to point out, it was essentially an
academic mind that welcomed Whitman so rapturously.

Less academic writers than Symonds were no less
rapturous. Oscar Wilde confessed: "I have an admiration
for that man which I can hardly express." For Stevenson,
Leaves of Grass "tumbled the world upside down."[14] Yeats
as a young man studied Whitman passionately, and under
his influence "sat talking in public bars, . . . talked late
into the night at many men's houses"; later he decided
that "intellectual freedom and social equality are in-
compatible," and that Whitman lacked the Vision of
Evil.[15] Perhaps the deepest affected of all the poets of this
time is also the most surprising, Gerard Manley Hopkins.

Surprising, that is, from the point of view of morality
and religious belief. Hopkins drew his priest's robes tight
around him when he confessed to Robert Bridges "that
I always knew in my heart Walt Whitman's mind to be
more like my own than any other man's living. As he is a
very great scoundrel this is not a pleasant confession. And
this also makes me the more desirous to read him and the
more determined that I will not."[16] The author of the
"Calamus" poems might well have disturbed the author
of "Harry Ploughman." In a letter to Bridges, Hopkins
called the poem "a direct picture of a ploughman, without afterthought. But when you read it let me know if
there is anything like it in Walt Whitman; as perhaps
there may be, and I should be sorry for that."[17]

In all respects of poetic practice, of language, rhythm,

H

and imagery, it is not, however, at all surprising that Hopkins was both attracted and alarmed by Whitman. They both thought of poetry in terms of language that is spoken. As Hopkins wrote to Bridges, criticising the archaism of Bridges' language, "it destroys earnest: we do not speak that way; therefore if a man speaks that way he is not serious, he is at something else than the seeming matter in hand."[18] Compare this with the Preface to the 1855 edition of *Leaves of Grass*: "I will not have in my writing any elegance, or effect, or originality, to hang in the way between me and the rest like curtains. I will have nothing hang in the way, not the richest curtains. What I tell I tell for precisely what it is."[19] Similarly, both poets thought of rhythm in terms of the speaking voice, although one expressed those rhythms instinctively and the other through a complex of theories. Compare "heaven-roysterers, in gay-gangs they throng; they glitter in marches"[20] with "Onward we move, a gay gang of blackguards! with mirth-shouting music and wild-flapping pennants of joy!"[21] Both refusing to compromise with current poetic diction, they met together under the hawk and the cloud. "Extremes meet, and (I must for truth's sake say what sounds pride) this savagery of [Whitman's] art, this rhythm in its last ruggedness and decomposition into common prose, comes near the last elaboration of mine."[22]

At the turn of the century, writings on Whitman tended to be either biographical or more concerned with him as a prophet than a poet. Fortunately, in 1914, a direct critical enquiry was at last turned on to Whitman's language and technique, in Basil de Selincourt's excellent *Walt Whitman, A Critical Study*. There is still no better discussion of Whitman's prosody. De Selincourt is sympathetic: Whitman "found by intuition the form which his genius required":[23] but he is also fully aware of the risks Whitman ran: "Unconfined, he is also unsustained."[24] Most important of all, perhaps, De Selincourt has made direct contact with that process of becoming that is at the heart of Whitman's poems, which gives them their extraordinary intimacy with the reader. As De Selincourt says, "We do more than read poetry. We feel it in its process and formation."[25] Yet the uncouthness and confusion that sometimes result do not indicate that Whitman is not a stylist. De Selincourt's words on this subject might well be enlarged in reference to include the self-imposed tortures of Hopkins' painfully conscious rebellion of technique:

> In so far as Whitman is a great stylist, it is not his daring unconventionalities that make him so, though these in themselves are such as to argue greatness of a kind. He is great because, having chosen his method, he takes the consequences of his choice with consummate pliability and responsiveness. He has been reflecting on the uses of language, and has struck out a line of his own for the use of it. In spite of this his writing is free from the taint of theory, has none of the rigidity of conscious rebellion, is not the less easy because he has determind to make it so.[26]

If England once more gave the lead, America fast caught up with her. American scholars have turned their rigorous attention to Whitman, with the result that, thanks to the work of Emory Holloway, C. J. Furness, and Gay Wilson Allen, there is now an excellent standard edition and definitive biography, as well as editions of uncollected poetry and prose, with variant readings of *Leaves of Grass* and selections with critical aids for students. This activity began in the nineteen-twenties; and it is ironic that by this time the two most eminent American literary expatriates, Ezra Pound and T. S. Eliot, had hardened their hearts against Whitman. Pound had condescendingly made a pact with Whitman, published in *Lustra* (1916), which reveals a great deal more than it says:

I make a pact with you, Walt Whitman—
I have detested you long enough.
I come to you as a grown child
Who has had a pig-headed father;
I am old enough now to make new friends.
It was you that broke the new wood,
Now it is a time for carving.
We have one sap and one root—
Let there be commerce between us.[27]

It is astounding that T. S. Eliot, in an introduction to a volume which reprints this poem, could write the following, in a discussion of *vers libre*:

To be precise, there are, for instance, my own type of verse, that of Pound, and that of the disciples of Whitman. I will not say that subsequently there have not appeared traces of reciprocal influence of several types upon one another, but I am here speaking of origins. My own verse is, so far as I can judge, nearer to the original meaning of *vers libre* than is any of the other types: at least, the form in which I began to write, in 1908 or 1909, was directly drawn from the study of Laforgue together with the later Elizabethan drama; and I do not know anyone who started from exactly that point. I did not read Whitman until much later in life, and had to conquer an aversion to his form, as well as to much of his matter, in order to do so. I am equally certain—it is indeed obvious—that Pound owes nothing to Whitman. This is an elementary observation. . . .[28]

Apparently, to Eliot the relation of a grown child to a pig-headed father is nothing. But then Eliot's rejection of America was as profound as Whitman's acceptance in his blood whether he likes it or not. Pound also made an intellectual and physical rejection of America, but at the same time preserved close ties with many aspects of American civilisation. Although America is basic, the

issues are far wider; Pound and Eliot have denied everything that Whitman affirmed in art. They have indig-
nantly repudiated in all their work Whitman's kidnapping of the Muse:

> Come Muse migrate from Greece and Ionia,
> Cross out please those immensely overpaid accounts,
> That matter of Troy and Achilles' wrath, and Aeneas',
>   Odysseus' wanderings,
> Placard "Removed" and "To Let" on the rocks of
>   your snowy Parnassus,
> Repeat at Jerusalem, place the notice high on Jaffa's
>   gate and on Mount Moriah,
> The same on the walls of your German, French and
>   Spanish castles, and Italian collections,
> For know a better, fresher, busier, sphere, a wide,
>   untried domain awaits, demands you.[29]

What else are Pound's *Cantos* but a pulling down of
Whitman's placards? Similarly, Pound and Eliot have
denied all Whitman's affirmations of hopeful democracy
and shared humanity. (If one had to make up a list of
improbable situations, high place might, perhaps, be
given to a picture of Pound or Eliot holding the hand of
a sick soldier in hospital.)

However, in the cadences of their long lines, in the
collation of apparently discordant material, and in the
use of imagery of sea-things and bird-song and lilac,
Pound and particularly Eliot seem to have been far
more influenced by Whitman than they have ever admitted in their prose writings. The whole subject in relation to Eliot has been convincingly surveyed, if at times
with excessive ingenuity, by S. Musgrove in *T. S. Eliot
and Walt Whitman*.

Where the majestic approach of "I, Walt Whitman"
sent Pound and Eliot scuttling for the door and the key,
D. H. Lawrence met him head on, greeting him with
alternate admiration and mockery. Lawrence saw from

the first how indissoluble were Whitman's form and content. "The clue to all his utterance lies in the sheer appreciation of the instant moment, life surging itself into utterance at its very well-head. . . . The quick of the universe is the *pulsating, carnal self*, mysterious and palpable. . . . Because Whitman put this into his poetry, we fear him and respect him profoundly."[30] Later Lawrence developed his ideas at more length in his essay on Whitman in *Studies in Classic American Literature*. He began with a ferociously witty blast against Whitman the orator, the apostle of merging and democracy, the man who aches with amorous love; this is all thoroughly enjoyable, as long as one remembers he is attacking only a part of Whitman. But in the second half of the essay—where he admits in a changed tone, "Whitman, the great poet, has meant so much to me. Whitman, the one man breaking a way ahead . . ."—Lawrence brilliantly establishes Whitman as a great moralist, as the carrier of "the American heroic message" that "the soul is not to pile up defences round herself . . . ," and as one honest enough to travel the open road to the edge of death.[31] Lawrence's essay is one of the most important discussions of Whitman available, but of course the entire body of his own work comprises the most eloquent witness of his regard for Whitman.

One of the great themes of Whitman's life and work is one to which William Blake gave supreme expression, innocence and experience. Whitman's incorruptibility, his health amidst sickness, his refusal to limit his responses, all combining in what Lawrence called "a morality of actual living, not of salvation," leave him, with all his experience, an innocence corresponding to the American dream. It is an infinitely moving innocence; it is only childish in that one would not want to see it hurt. But hurt it is; and some of Whitman's greatest poetry, such as "Out of the Cradle endlessly rocking," comes from this hurt. Whitman, like Blake,

saw innocence in the city street; the most extraordinary
witness to the pathos of the innocent poet in the corrupt
city is the Spanish poet Federico Garcia Lorca, who
came to New York in the full horror of the depression
years, in 1929. He sees the poet of pure, comradely love
surrounded with surrealist images of perversion:

New York of mud
New York of wires and death.
What angel do you carry hidden in your cheek?
What perfect voice will speak the truths of wheat?
And who the terrible dream of your stained anemones?

Not for a single moment, handsome old Walt Whitman,
have I lost the vision of your beard full of butterflies,
your corduroy shoulders wasted by the moon
your thighs of virginal Apollo,
your voice like a column of coarse ashes;
old man beautiful as mist,
who moaned like a bird
whose sex is run through by a needle,
enemy of the satyr,
enemy of the vine
and lover of bodies under coarse cloth.
Not for a single moment, manly handsome one,
who on mountains of coal, advertisements and railroads
dreamed of being a river and sleeping like a river
with that comrade who set in your heart
a little pain of an ignorant leopard.

Not for a single moment, Adam, blood-brother, male,
man alone in the sea, handsome old Walt Whitman,
for the reason that on the rooftops,
or crowded together in bars,
leaping in bunches from the drains,
trembling between the legs of drivers
or gyrating on platforms of absinthe
the queers, Walt Whitman, marking you down!
. . . queers of the cities,

with tumescent flesh and filthy minds,
bitches, harpies, sleepless enemies
of the Love that distributes crowns of joy. . . .

. . . Agony, agony, dream, ferment, dream.
This is the world, old friend, agony, agony.
The dead decompose under the city clocks,
war goes weeping on with a million grey rats,
the rich bestow on their darlings
little illuminated gifts of death
and life is not noble, nor good, nor sacred. . . .

. . . And you, beautiful Walt Whitman, sleep on by the
     banks of the Hudson,
with your beard towards the pole and your hands
     outspread.
Pliant clay or snow, your tongue is summoning
comrades to guard your gazelle that has no body.
Sleep on; nothing lasts.
A dance of walls agitates the meadows
and American submerges itself under machines and a
     flood of tears.
I wish that a strong breeze from profoundest night
would take away flowers and letters from the arch
     where you sleep,
and a black boy announce to the golden whites
the coming of the kingdom of the ear of corn.[32]

Lorca apprehended with a true poet's insight the battle
between innocence and perversion, fertility and sterility,
which Whitman's poetry now has to fight, as indeed it
had to fight to achieve existence. Lorca understood
Whitman far better than his strident but uneasy disciple,
Hart Crane. The painful passage in "The Bridge," where
the homosexual Crane holds hands with Whitman, not
for love but because Whitman was the singer of steel and
bridges, brought the wrath of Crane's friend Yvor Winters
down on poor Whitman. To read Winters' *In Defense of
Reason* one would think that Whitman was nothing but a

ratbag orator with a fatuous belief in progress and change whose so-called verse represents nothing but a huge heap of rock from which an ounce or two of gold might be refined by an engineer of genius. And Allen Tate and R. P. Blackmur have been as hostile as Winters.[33]

However, in America in the nineteen-fifties there was a notable warming of sympathy towards Whitman. Richard V. Chase's *Walt Whitman Reconsidered* is the best modern book about the poet and his work. Chase has had the nerve to write about Whitman lovingly: but he has also been constantly nervous of the critical opposition around the corner, and this has made him hunt for fashionable ingredients, such as wit, to the detriment of other equally important qualities in Whitman. Nevertheless, it is a just and well-informed book, and its caution is needed at this stage in Whitman's poetical reputation. Apart from Chase's book, much the best full treatment of Whitman is in F. O. Matthiessen's *American Renaissance*. Matthiessen devotes over 110 pages to Whitman's language and rhythms, and to the relation between the poet's vision and the sights and sounds of his favourite haunts. Both Matthiessen and Chase are well aware of the importance of Whitman's prose writings, and their analyses of his verse in its subtlety and strength, in its determination to break down the barriers between prose and poetry, give further weight to De Selincourt's thesis that Whitman is a great stylist. Perhaps Edmund Wilson has expressed the crux of this question of Whitman's style most neatly of all: "The effort to apply to Whitman the ordinary standards of verse has hindered the appreciation of his careful and exquisite art."[34]

The collection of essays edited by Milton Hindus, *Leaves of Grass, One Hundred Years after*, is distinctly irregular in quality, but those by Hindus himself, Richard Chase (incorporated in his book on Whitman), David Daiches, and particularly Leslie A. Fiedler, re-establish Whitman firmly on ground that he should never have lost. Once again, one cannot help being amused by the wary tone which those who would defend Whitman had to adopt in the nineteen-fifties.

Whitman has had some odd disciples in his time, but none odder or more remote from his own prudent, middle class nature than the Beat Generation. The open rhythms and all-inclusive catalogues of Allen Ginsberg's *Howl* certainly make an example of the Whitman tradition taken to an extreme, but the poetic identity it creates, that of a hopeless, promiscuous, partially insane junkie "looking for an angry fix," would have shocked and repelled the Whitman who struggled to achieve sanity and health. As Kenneth Rexroth and others have pointed out, Whitman's influence is clear and gladly accepted amongst the young American poets who are outside the academic circles. These, as described by Rexroth, would have revolted Whitman as much as the wildest Beatnik. "The entire educational system is a conspiracy to make poetry as unpalatable as possible. From the seventh grade teacher who rolls her eyes and chants H.D. to the seven types of ambiguity factories, grinding out little Donnes and Hopkinses with hayseeds in their hair, everybody is out to de-poetize forever the youth of the land."[35]

In an interesting short essay Malcolm Cowley has discussed that mysterious period of Whitman's life, covering the six years from the first edition of *Leaves of Grass* in 1855, in terms of eastern philosophy and a rejection of contemporary convention, both prime articles in the Beatnik faith. "Much of his conduct," writes Cowley, "also resembled that of the Beat Generation. He stayed out of the rat race, he avoided the squares, preferring the company of omnibus drivers and deckhands on the ferries; he was 'real gone,' he was 'far out'; and he was writing poems in what Lawrence Lipton calls 'the open, free-swinging style that is prized in Beat Generation literature'!"[36]

The result of all this revival of interest in Whitman is that now, in the nineteen-sixties, one can at least praise him without being thought a fanatical disciple, and criticise him without pretending that he is not a poet at all.

For the true survival of literature, apart from its academic study, each age must be ruthlessly selfish about the poetry of the past. It must say, "What is in this for *me*?" (This should *not* mean: "Is there a Ph.D. or an article in *PMLA* in it for me?" though, alas, it often does.) Living literature is perpetually putting down new roots, and it is as sensitive as a camellia to lime; a forcing into the wrong soil will kill it. However, a great writer is continental, there is enough in him to support all different kinds of growth. Whitman is such a great writer, whose vastness contains qualities of epic and myth as well as extreme sophistication. Moreover, a great deal of his poetry is about the process of becoming, and this has made it peculiarly relevant to the social and individual developments of our time, increasing its greatness. Whitman himself saw how the quality of literature is involved with its growth in time.

No really great song can ever attain full purport till long after the death of its singer—till it has accrued and incorporated the many passions, many joys and sorrows, it has itself arous'd.[37]

As the Prophet of Democracy, Whitman is rightly suspect: but as an observable specimen, as part of the very growth of democracy, he is not. As Sir Winston Churchill remarked, democracy seems impossible, until you examine the other systems. If we are obliged to live with it, and in the nineteen-sixties this seems an elementary obligation, we should be grateful for anyone who can help us understand it at the very well-springs of its origins in human identity. This is Whitman's great subject, in life as in literature, in the best of his prose as well as in his verse. Ideas, however, will go nowhere without language; here Whitman is again relevant, as his attempts both to "Make it New" and to keep poetry close to living speech have resulted in a poetic language that seems to have been freshly spoken. His "language experiment" paid off. Thanks to the work of recent criticism, no one now need be put off by the caricature of Whitman as a humourless, simple-minded believer in inevitable progress. His doubts go as deep as his fundamentally comic view of himself. Whitman would refuse to share the pessimism of a Camus, but he had already admitted the absurd as part of human identity, and he would certainly agree that each man carries the microbe of the plague within him. Taking all this into account, Whitman still has the temerity to affirm. As Randall Jarrell has said in an excellent essay: "They might have put on his tombstone WALT WHITMAN: HE HAD HIS NERVE." The child who asked the poet "What is the grass?" was answered first by: "I guess it must be the flag of my disposition, out of hopeful green stuff woven." The poet went on to say that it was many other things as well, but as for the further question, "What is *Leaves of Grass*?", the poet can answer best himself, even though he is talking about the Bible, in an essay called (significantly for Whitman's verse) "The Bible as Poetry":

The metaphors daring beyond account, the lawless soul, extravagant by our standards, the glow of love and friendship, the fervent kiss—nothing in argument or logic, but unsurpass'd in proverbs, in religious ecstasy, in suggestions of common mortality and death, man's great equalizers—the spirit everything, the ceremonies and forms of the churches nothing, faith limitless, its immense sensuousness immensely spiritual —an incredible, all-inclusive non-worldliness and dew-scented illiteracy (the antipodes of our Nineteenth

Century business absorption and morbid refinement)
—no hair-splitting doubts, no sickly sulking and sniff-
ling, no *Hamlet*, no "Adonais," no "Thanatopsis," no
"In Memoriam." . . . Even to our Nineteenth Century
here are our fountain heads of song.[38]

And, with Whitman, even to our Twentieth Century.

REFERENCES

1. Introduction to Ezra Pound, *Selected Poems*, London 1928, p. xi.
2. *Leaves of Grass One Hundred Years After*, ed. M. Hindus, Stanford and London 1955, p. 71.
3. *Complete Verse and Selected Prose and Letters*, ed. Holloway, pp. 1000–2.
4. *W.W.C.*, IV. 267.
5. Charles Eliot Norton, *A Leaf of Grass from Shady Hill, With a Review of Walt Whitman's Leaves of Grass* (1855), Mass., Cambridge, 1928.
6. 15 Mar. 1856.
7. Quoted in Kincheloe, *British Periodical Criticism of American Literature*, 1851–1870 (unpublished thesis, Duke University), p. 310.
8. Quoted in *op. cit.*, p. 209.
9. Quoted in *op. cit.*, p. 219.
10. *The Swinburne Letters*, ed. Cecil Y. Lang, VOL. I, New Haven and London 1959, p. 58.
11. "To Walt Whitman in America." *Collected Poetical Works*, London 1924, VOL. I, p. 780.
12. *Under the Microscope*, London 1872, p. 47.
13. *Walt Whitman, a Study*, London 1893, pp. 157–60.
14. Quoted in *Leaves of Grass One Hundred Years After*, ed. Hindus, p. 10.
15. Yeats, *Autobiographies*, p. 246.
16. *The Letters of Gerard Manley Hopkins to Robert Bridges*, ed. C.C. Abbott, London 1935, p. 155.
17. *Op. cit.*, p. 262.
18. *Op. cit.*, p. 218.
19. *C.W.*, V. 171.
20. "That Nature is a Heraclitean Fire," in *Poems of Gerard Manley Hopkins*, ed. R. Bridges, 3rd edn., London 1948, p. 111.
21. "The Sleepers." *C.W.*, II. 203.
22. *The Letters of Gerard Manley Hopkins to Robert Bridges*, ed. Abbott, p. 157.
23. *Walt Whitman, a Critical Study*, London 1914, p. 91.
24. *Op. cit.*, p. 83.
25. *Op. cit.*, p. 114.

26. *Op. cit.*, pp. 152–3.
27. *Selected Poems*, 1928, p. 72.
28. *Op. cit.*, pp. viii–ix.
29. "Song of the Exposition." *C.W.*, I. 238–9.
30. Introduction to *New Poems*, 1920. Reprinted in *Selected Literary Criticism*, ed. Beal, p. 87.
31. *Selected Literary Criticism*, pp. 392 ff.
32. "Ode to Walt Whitman," printed in *Poet in New York*, tr. G. Dutton.
33. R. P. Blackmur, *Language as Gesture*, New York 1952, p. 31.
34. Edmund Wilson, *The Triple Thinkers*, London 1952, p. 31.
35. *Protest*, edd. G. Feldman and M. Gastenberg, p. 280.
36. *New Republic*, 26 Oct. 1959.
37. "The Bible as Poetry." *C.W.*, VI. 108.
38. *C.W.*, VI. 105–6.

SELECT BIBLIOGRAPHY

I. WHITMAN'S WORKS

1. Verse

Leaves of Grass. Brooklyn 1855, 94 pp.; 2nd edn., Brooklyn (Fowler and Wells, 1856, 384 pp.; 3rd edn., Boston (Thayer and Eldridge) 1860, 456 pp.; 4th edn., New York 1867, 338 pp.; 5th edn., 384 pp., and *Passage to India*, 120 pp., in one volume Washington 1871; 6th edn., Washington 1872; 7th edn. (Author's Centennial), Camden, reprint of 5th edn.; 8th edn., Boston (James R. Osgood and Co.) 1881, 382 pp.; 9th edn. (Author's Edition) issued by Whitman 1882 from Osgood's plates, later published by Rees, Welch and Co., Philadelphia, later published by David McKay, Philadelphia; 10th edn. (containing *Sands at Seventy, Good-Bye, My Fancy*), Philadelphia (David McKay) 1891.

November Boughs. Philadelphia (David McKay) 1888.

Complete Poems and Prose of Walt Whitman . . . Containing Sands at Seventy and November Boughs. Philadelphia (David McKay) 1888.

2. Prose

Democratic Vistas. Washington 1871.

Two Rivulets, Prose and Verse. Camden 1876.

Specimen Days and Collect. Philadelphia (Rees, Welch and Co.) 1882.

Complete Prose Works. Philadelphia (David McKay) 1892.

3. Collections, Selections and Reprints

The Complete Writings of Walt Whitman, edd. R. M. Bucke, T. N. Harned and Horace L. Traubel. New York and London 1902. 10 vols.

Uncollected Poetry and Prose of Walt Whitman, ed. Emory Holloway. New York 1932. 2 vols.

Walt Whitman, Complete Poetry & Selected Prose and Letters, ed. Emory Holloway. London (Nonesuch Press) 1938.

With Walt Whitman in Camden, by Horace L. Traubel. VOL. I: *March 29–July 14, 1888*, Boston 1906; VOL. II: *July 16–October 31, 1888*, New York 1908; VOL. III: *November 1, 1888–January 20, 1889*, New York 1914; VOL. IV: *January 21–April 7, 1889*, Philadelphia 1953.

Walt Whitman's Workshop, ed. Clifton Joseph Furness. Cambridge, Mass., 1928.

Walt Whitman's Leaves of Grass, The First (1855) Edition, ed. with an introduction by Malcolm Cowley. New York (Viking Press) and London (Secker and Warburg) 1959.

The Complete Poetry and Prose of Walt Whitman, with an introduction by Malcolm Cowley. Garden City, New York, 1954.

Walt Whitman's Poems, Selections with Critical Aids, edd. G. W. Allen and C. T. Davis. New York (Grove Press) and London (John Calder) 1959.

The Correspondence of Walt Whitman, VOLS. I & II, ed. Edwin H. Miller. New York (N.Y. U.P.) 1961.

II. BOOKS AND ARTICLES ABOUT WHITMAN

ALLEN, GAY WILSON. *The Solitary Singer: A Critical Biography of Walt Whitman*. New York, The Macmillan Co., 1955; reprinted as a paperback, New York, Grove Press, London, John Calder, n.d.

ANON. "The Bird of Freedom," middle essay in *T.L.S.*, 2 Jun. 1961.

ASSELINEAU, ROGER. *The Evolution of Walt Whitman*. Cambridge, Mass. (Harvard U.P.) and London (Oxford U.P.) 1961.

BINNS, HENRY B. *A Life of Walt Whitman*. London 1905.

CANBY, HENRY S. *Walt Whitman, an American: A Study in Biography*. Boston 1943.

CATEL, JEAN. *Rythme et langage dans la 1re édition des Leaves of Grass*. Paris 1930.

CHASE, RICHARD V. *Walt Whitman Reconsidered*. London 1955.

COWLEY, MALCOLM. "The Guru, the Beatnik and the Good Gray Poet," in *The New Republic*, 26 Oct. 1959.

DAICHES, DAVID. *Poetry and the Modern World*. Chicago 1940.

—— Essay on Whitman in *The Young Rebel in American Literature*, ed. Carl Bode, London 1959.

ELIOT, T. S. Introduction to *Selected Poems* by Ezra Pound, London 1934.

HINDUS, MILTON (ed.). *Leaves of Grass, One Hundred Years After.* Stanford and London 1955.

HOLLOWAY, EMORY. *Whitman: An Interpretation in Narrative.* New York 1926.

JARRELL, RANDALL. "Some Lines from Whitman," in *Poetry and the Age*, New York 1953.

JEFFARES, A. NORMAN. "Walt Whitman: The Barbaric Yawp," in *The Great American Experiment*, ed. Carl Bode. London (Heinemann) 1961.

KINCHELOE, H. G. *British Periodical Criticism of American Literature, 1851–1870*, Unpublished Duke University Thesis.

LAWRENCE, D. H. *Selected Literary Criticism*, ed. Anthony Beal. London 1955, New York 1956.

LEAVIS, F. R. *New Bearings in English Poetry.* London 1950. Ann Arbor, Michigan, 1960.

LORCA, FEDERICO GARCIA. "Ode to Walt Whitman," in *Poet in New York*, London n.d., New York 1955.

MATTHIESSEN, F. O. *American Renaissance.* New York 1941.

MILLER (JR.), JAMES E. *A Critical Guide to Leaves of Grass.* Chicago 1957.

MUSGROVE, S. *T. S. Eliot and Walt Whitman.* Wellington, New Zealand, 1952.

PERRY, BLISS. *Walt Whitman: His Life and Work.* Boston 1906.

SELINCOURT, BASIL DE. *Walt Whitman, A Critical Study.* London 1914.

SITWELL, EDITH. Pref. in *The American Genius: An Anthology. . . .* London 1951.

SYMONDS, JOHN ADDINGTON. *Walt Whitman, A Study.* London and New York 1893.

Walt Whitman Review, The. Wayne State University, Detroit, Michigan. Lists current publications and publishes scholarly and critical essays on Whitman.